A Frantic Assembly and State Theatre Company
South Australia production.

Originally co-produced with Warwick Arts Centre
in association with Chichester Festival Theatre and
the Lyric Hammersmith

Things I know to be True

by Andrew Bovell

This production of *Things I Know to be True* was
revived on 27 September 2017 at Oxford Playhouse,
before touring the UK

Photography © Helen Maybanks

CREATIVE TEAM

Writer — Andrew Bovell
Directors — Geordie Brookman & Scott Graham
Set & Lighting Designer — Geoff Cobham
Costume Designer — Ailsa Paterson
Sound Designer — Andrew Howard
Casting Director — Sarah Hughes
Associate Director — Jonnie Riordan

Featuring the music of Nils Frahm
Original artwork by Thomas Buchanan

CAST

Mark Price — Matthew Barker
Fran Price — Cate Hamer
Pip Price — Seline Hizli
Bob Price — John McArdle
Rosie Price — Kirsty Oswald
Ben Price — Arthur Wilson

PRODUCTION TEAM

Production Manager — Ali Beale
Company Stage Manager — Julia Reid
Technical Stage Manager — Simon Legg
Deputy Stage Manager — Emma Rangel
Production LX — Tom White
Re-lighter — Matt O'Leary
Associate Sound Designer & Production Engineer — Rob Parkinson
Costume Supervisor — Marny Clulow

FOR FRANTIC ASSEMBLY

Artistic Director — Scott Graham
Interim Executive Director — Julie Weston
Producer — Anna Moutrey
Associate Director — Neil Bettles
Head of Learning & Participation — Sharon Kanolik
General Manager — Fiona Gregory
Associate Director (Learning & Participation) — Simon Pittman
Ignition Project Manager — Scarlett Spiro-Beazley
Learning & Participation Coordinator — Juliet Styles

FOR STATE THEATRE COMPANY

Executive Director/Producer	Jodi Glass
Artistic Director	Geordie Brookman
Resident Artist	Elena Carapetis
Resident Designer	Geoff Cobham
Resident Sound Designer & Head of Audio	Andrew Howard
Artistic Program Manager	Shelley Lush
Youth & Education Manager	Kimberley Martin
Marketing Manager	Jemma Knight
Marketing Coordinator:	Cat Turner
Media & Communications Manager	Lindsay Ferris
Graphic Design & Digital Producer	Robin Mather
Philanthropy Coordinator	Bernadette Woods
Events & Database Coordinator	Ben Roberts
Finance Manager	Natalie Loveridge
Artistic & Finance Administrator	Fiona Lukac
Production Manager	Gavin Norris
Deputy Production Manager	Gabrielle Hornhardt
Props Coordinator	Stuart Crane
Production Trainee	Alira McKenzie-Williams
Workshop Supervisor	John Meyer
Leading Hand	Areste Nicola
Carpenter & Prop Maker	Patrick Duggin
Carpenter/Metal Worker:	Guy Bottroff
Scenic Art:	Sandra Anderson
Head Electrician	Sue Grey-Gardner
Workshop	Michael Ambler
Prop Shop	Robin Balogh
Head of Wardrobe	Kellie Jones
Wardrobe Production Supervisor/Buyer	Enken Hagge
Costume Maker/Cutter	Martine Micklem
Hair, Make-Up, Wigs & Costume Hire	Jana Debiasi
Overseas Representatives (London)	Henny Finch
Overseas Representative (New York)	Stuart Thompson

Public Relations: The Corner Shop / www.cornershoppr.com
Marketing & Sales Directors: Joe Public / www.joepublicmarketing.com

Thanks to

DIRECTORS' NOTE

It's a delight for both of us to be restaging Andrew's beautiful play for a third time and bringing it to an even wider UK audience. When we started discussing a possible cross hemisphere collaboration in 2013 we never imagined that the resulting work might play to more than 40,000 people across the two halves of the globe and have such impact upon its audience.

Both Frantic Assembly and State Theatre Company South Australia are companies that are proud to place the value of storytelling ahead of everything else and in Andrew's writing we perhaps found the perfect meeting point. But in the core creative team we also found a depth of collaboration that is rare and precious. The group of makers involved have, over the course of the three evolving productions, become an extended family of sorts and it is in family that the play itself finds its emotive focus.

Andrew's writing is always, in one way or another, about our struggle to love and how we can hurt those close to us with a kind of precision guided impact that is beyond us with anyone else. In *Things I Know To Be True* he asks us, what do the generations owe each other? Can the 'sacrifice now live later' ethos of our parents generation ever find a happy meeting point with the 'live now' approach of the millenials? Most of all he looks at the tightness of the ties that bind and how we must face our parents' imperfections as part of facing our own.

Geordie Brookman & Scott Graham

CREATIVE TEAM

Andrew Bovell (Writer)

Andrew Bovell is a critically acclaimed Australian playwright and screenwriter.

His recent theatre credits include *The Secret River* (Sydney Theatre Company, 2013 Sydney Festival, 2016 national tour, 2017 Adelaide Festival; winner of six Helpmann Awards); *When the Rain Stops Falling* (Brink Production/State Theatre Company, 2008 Adelaide Festival; Almeida Theatre, Lincoln Centre NYC, winner of five Lucille Lortell Awards). Earlier works include *Speaking in Tongues*, *Holy Day* and *Who's Afraid of the Working Class*.

Film credits include *Iris*, *A Most Wanted Man*, *Edge of Darkness*, *Blessed*, *Lantana*, *Head On* and *Strictly Ballroom*.

Geordie Brookman (Co-Director)

Geordie Brookman is the Artistic Director of State Theatre Company South Australia.

For State Theatre Company, his directing credits include *Macbeth*, *A Doll's House*, *Betrayal*, *Summer of the Seventeenth Doll*, *The Importance of Being Earnest*, *Little Bird*, *The Seagull*, *Hedda Gabler*, *The Kreutzer Sonata*, *Speaking in Tongues*, *romeo&juliet*, *Knives In Hens* (with Malthouse), *Ghosts*, *Attempts on Her Life*, *Toy Symphony* (with Queensland Theatre Company). For Sydney Theatre Company: *Spring Awakening: The Musical*, *Machu Picchu*, *Kryptonite*. For Belvoir: *Baghdad Wedding*, *Tender*, *Disco Pigs*.

Geordie's productions have won or been nominated for Helpmann, Greenroom, Sydney Critics Circle and Adelaide Critics Circle Awards.

Scott Graham (Co-Director)

Scott Graham is Artistic Director and co-founder of Frantic Assembly.

For Frantic Assembly he recently directed *Fatherland*, *No Way Back*, *Othello* and *The Believers*. Other Frantic Assembly credits include co-directing *Little Dogs, Lovesong, Beautiful Burnout* and *Stockholm*.

Other directing credits include *Man to Man* (Wales Millennium Centre); *Home* (National Theatre of Scotland).

Scott received Olivier and Tony Award nominations for his choreography on *The Curious Incident of the Dog in the Night-Time* (National Theatre).

He has, with Steven Hoggett, written The Frantic Assembly Book of Devising Theatre (Routledge 2nd ed.).

Scott is Visiting Professor in Theatre Practice at Coventry University.

Geoff Cobham (Set & Lighting Designer)

Geoff Cobham is State Theatre Company's Resident Designer and has worked as a Production Manager, Lighting Designer, Set Designer, Event Producer and Venue Designer.

For State Theatre Company, his recent Set & Lighting Design includes *A Doll's House, The 39 Steps, Things I Know To Be True, The Events, Betrayal, Little Bird, The Seagull, Hedda Gabler, The Kruetzer Sonata.* Other Set & Lighting Design credits include: *Nothing to Lose, Never Did Me Any Harm, The Age I'm In* (Force Majeure).

His recent Lighting Design credits for State Theatre Company include *Mortido, Volpone,*

He received a Helpmann Award for Best Scenic Design of the production of *Little Bird.*

Ailsa Paterson (Costume Designer)

Ailsa Paterson completed the Bachelor of Dramatic Art in Design (NIDA) in 2003.

For State Theatre Company, her Set and Costume Design credits include *A Doll's House, The 39 Steps, Mendelssohn's Dream* (with the Adelaide Symphony Orchestra), *Betrayal, Beckett Triptych (Footfalls, Eh Joe, Krapp's Last Tape), The Importance of Being Earnest, Hedda Gabler, In the Next Room or The Vibrator Play.* Other theatre design credits include *Cloudstreet!* (Costume Design, State Opera of SA); *Naturally* (Restless); *The Streets* (OzAsia Festival 2015); *Cranky Bear* (Patch); *Mouse, Bird and Sausage* (Costume Design, Slingsby); *Other Desert Cities, Seminar* and *Skylight* (Ensemble).

Ailsa received the 2011 Mike Walsh Fellowship.

Andrew Howard (Sound Designer)

Andrew Howard has worked as a composer, sound designer and sound engineer since 2000. He was a founding member of The Border Project.

He is Resident Sound Designer for State Theatre Company, his sound design credits include *A Soll'd House, Sista Girl, Machu Picchu, This Is Where We Live, Kryptonite, Maggie Stone, Babyteeth, The Comedy of Errors* (head of audio), *Random, The Kreutzer Sonata, romeo&juliet, Knives in Hens* and *Attempts on Her Life.*

His other theatre credits as Sound Designer and/or Composer include *Despoiled Shore, Medeamaterial, Landscape with Argonauts, The War, Please Go Hop, Highway Rock 'n' Roll Disaster, Trouble on Planet Earth* and *Disappearance* (The Border Project).

Nils Frahm (Featured Music)

Nils Frahm is a musician, composer and record producer.

Musician credits include *Wintermusik* (2009), *The Bells* (2009), *Felt* (2011), *Juno Screws* (2012), *Juno Reworked* (2013 with guest reworks by Luke Abbott and Clark), *Spaces* (2013), *Collaborative Works* (2015 in collaboration with Ólafur Arnalds).

He created the score for the film *Victoria* (2015), which won the German film prize for Best Soundtrack.

Nils is part of Piano Day. An official body created by Nils and friends to celebrate the piano and to house various and exciting, piano-related projects.

He has also published published two music books, *Sheets Eins* and *Sheets Zwei*.

Sarah Hughes (Casting Director)

Sarah Hughes is Alan Ayckbourn's casting director and has also freelanced extensively for the Entertainment Department of the BBC.

Theatre credits include plays for the West Yorkshire Playhouse, Birmingham Rep, Manchester Royal Exchange, Theatre Royal Northampton, and multiple productions for Frantic Assembly, Stafford Shakespeare Festival, the Stephen Joseph Theatre Scarborough, and Graeae.

Jonnie Riordan (Associate Director)

Jonnie Riordan is a graduate of Frantic Assembly's Ignition. He is Associate Director of ThickSkin and a creative practitioner for Frantic Assembly.

Movement Director credits include *Eyes Closed Ears Covered* (Bunker); Connections Festival (National Theatre); *Maggie & Pierre* (Finborough); *Mobile* (The Paper Birds); *Home* (Frozen Light); *CAUGHT* (Pleasance); *A Tale of Two Cities* (Brit Project, University of South Florida). As Associate Movement Director: *Whisper House* (The Other Palace); *Myth (RSC)*.

Directing credits include *Man Up* (Frantic Assembly Ignition), *Boy Magnet, White Noise* (ThickSkin). Associate Director; *Chalk Farm, The Static* (ThickSkin).

Performer credits include *This Will All Be Gone, No Way Back, Canticles* (Frantic Assembly); *Full Stop* (Light The Fuse); *Boy Magnet* (ThickSkin); *The Marriage of Figaro* (Opera Holland Park); *The Fear* (Frantic Assembly's Ignition).

Photography © Helen Maybanks

CAST

Matthew Barker (Mark Price)
Matthew Barker trained at the Royal Scottish Academy of Music and Drama.

Previous work with Frantic Assembly includes *The Curious Incident of the Dog in the Night-Time* (National Theatre).

Theatre credits include *Husbands & Sons, NT50, 13, Emperor and Galilean, Hamlet* (National Theatre); *Good People* (Hampstead); *Much Ado About Nothing* (Derby LIVE).

Television credits include *The Lost Honour of Christopher Jefferies* (Carnival Films); *Doctors, EastEnders* (BBC); *Jericho: The Killing of Johnny Swan* (Granada); *No Angels* (World Productions/Channel 4).

Cate Hamer (Fran Price)
Theatre credits include *The National Joke, The Swing of Things* (Stephen Joseph Theatre); *Suddenly Last Summer, Abigail's Party, Enlightenment* (Theatre by the Lake); *Crime and Punishment, A Christmas Carol* (Glasgow Citizens); *A Bed Amongst the Lentils* (West Yorkshire Playhouse); *The Heretic, Arcadia* (Lowry, Manchester); *Rock 'n' Roll, Larkin With Woman, Beyond Belief: Shipman Enquiry* (Manchester Library Theatre); *Way Upstream, The Country, Indian Ink* (Salisbury Playhouse); *Brighton Beach Memoirs, The Beauty Queen of Leenane* (Watford Palace); *A Midsummer Night's Dream* (Shakespeare's Globe tour); *Scenes from an Execution* (Hackney Empire Studio); *A House of Correction* (The Wrestling School); *A Conversation, Across Oka, Rafts and Dreams* (Manchester Royal Exchange); *Les Liaisons Dangereuses* (Bristol Old Vic); *As You Like It* (Nottingham Playhouse); *Dona Rosita, The Tower, Volpone* (Almeida); *Machinal* (National Theatre); *Love of the Nightingale, Mary and Lizzie, The Tempest* (RSC).

Television includes *EastEnders, The Town, When I'm 64, Without Motive, The Rainbow, Inspector Lynley Mysteries, Holby City, Coronation Street, Casualty, The Bill, Doctors, The Practice.*

Seline Hizli (Pip Price)
Theatre credits include *One Night in November, Blood Wedding, House of Bernarda Alba, Jumpy* (inc West End transfer); *In The Republic of Happiness* (Royal Court); *Dirty Butterfly* (Young Vic) and *Women on the Verge of a Nervous Breakdown* (ATG).

Television credits include *Land Girls, Appropriate Adult, Call the Midwife, Luther, Mum* and the series regular of Margaret in *Grantchester* for ITV.

Seline will be next seen in the second series of *Mum* for the BBC.

John McArdle (Bob Price)

Theatre credits include *Lennon* (Liverpool Everyman); *Our Country's Good* (Liverpool Playhouse); *Two, An Enemy of the People, Oh! What A Lovely War* (Bolton Octagon); *The Crucible* (Sheffield Crucible); *Brassed Off* (York Theatre Royal/national tour); *The Arbour* (National Theatre); *The Rise and Fall of Little Voice* (tour); *Flying Blind* (Manchester Library Theatre); *Accidental Death of an Anarchist* (Contact, Manchester).

Television credits include *Brookside* (regular character); *Gallowglass, City Central, Merseybeat, Casualty, Holby City, Waterloo Road, New Tricks* (BBC1); *The Cazalets, Waking the Dead, Seaforth* (BBC 2); *Law & Order UK, UB Dead, Blue Murder, Prime Suspect 5, Finney, Vera, Emmerdale* (regular) (ITV); *The Beat Goes On* (Channel 4).

Film credits include *There's Only One Jimmy Grimble, The Place of The Dead, The Revenger's Tragedy, Charlie Noades, Skallergrig, Rich Deceiver, Through My Eyes, Rochdale Pioneers.*

Radio credits include *A Clockwork Orange, The Spire, King of the Hill, and Stockport So Good They Named It Once* (BBC Radio 4).

Kirsty Oswald (Rosie Price)

Previous work for Frantic Assembly includes *Othello* (2014 UK tour).

Theatre credits include *The Father* (Wyndham's); *We Are Proud To Present...* (Bush); *The Winter's Tale* (Sheffield Crucible); *The Judas Kiss* (Hampstead/Duke of York's).

Television credits include *Beowulf* (ITV); *Ripper Street* (Tiger Aspect); *The Coroner, Holby City, Sadie J* (BBC); *Salting the Battlefield* (Carnival); *Dancing on the Edge* (Ruby Films).

Film credits include *Le Weekend* (Poisson Rouge); *Gutterdammerung* (Gun Productions); *A Little Chaos* (Potboiler).

Radio credits include *The Power and the Glory, The Forsytes, Moll Flanders* (BBC).

Arthur Wilson (Ben Price)

Theatre credits include *Persuasion* (Manchester Royal Exchange); *The Crunch* (Look Left Look Right); *Richard II* (Shakespeare's Globe); *Man and Superman* (National Theatre); *The Comedy of Errors, A Midsummer Night's Dream, The Taming of the Shrew, Twelfth Night* (Propeller Theatre Company world tours); *Project Space* (Secret Cinema); *Peter Pan* (Kensington Gardens, O2 & US tour); *Resurrection* (Òran Mór); *Hard Times, If I Were You, Tom's Midnight Garden* (Library, Manchester); *Home – Edinburgh* (National Theatre of Scotland); *Amid the Clouds* (Tron); *The Borrowers* (Citizens).

Televison credits include *Call The Midwife* (BBC); *Law and Order* (Kudos); *20 Anything (*Comedy Unit); *The Academy* (2act); *Sea of Souls* (BBC).

TRACK LIST

It Was Really, Really Grey
More
Stolen Car
Keep
Tristana
Snippet
Said and Done
Corn
Ambre
For Peter – Toilet Brushes – More Less

Written by Nils Frahm
Published by Manners McDade Music Publishing Ltd.
Administered by Hebbes Music Group

Photography © Helen Maybanks

FRANTIC ASSEMBLY

Award-winning theatre company Frantic Assembly's method of devising theatre has been impacting theatrical practice and unlocking the creative potential of future theatre-makers for twenty-three years.

One of the most exciting theatre companies in the UK, Frantic Assembly is led by Artistic Director and co-founder Scott Graham, and has toured extensively across Great Britain, and worked in over forty countries internationally collaborating with some of today's most inspiring artists.

Frantic Assembly is currently studied as a leading contemporary theatre practitioner on five British and international academic syllabuses. The success of the company's distinct approach has influenced contemporary theatre-making and foregrounded the use of movement directors and choreographers in new dramatic works. With a history of commissioning writers such as Mark Ravenhill, Abi Morgan, Simon Stephens and Bryony Lavery the company has been acclaimed for its collaborative approach. In 2016 the company started delivering practical modules on a new Collaborative Theatre-Making MA it has created with Coventry University (UK Modern University of the Year 2014, 2015, 2016 and UK University of the Year 2015). Frantic Assembly runs Ignition, a free national training programme for young men aged 16–20, increasing involvement in and access to the arts in places of low cultural engagement.

Frantic Assembly productions include *Fatherland*, *Things I Know To be True* (UK and Australia), *Othello*, *Beautiful Burnout* (UK, Australia, New Zealand and New York), *Lovesong*, *Stockholm* (UK and Australia), *The Believers*. They are also the Movement Directors on the award-winning National Theatre of Great Britain, production *The Curious Incident of the Dog in the Night-Time* (West End, Broadway, UK & Ireland tour, US tour). Television credits include Movement Direction on BAFTA winning British–American series *Humans* (AMC, Channel 4 & Kudos).

www.franticassembly.co.uk

twitter @franticassembly
instagram @frantic_assembly
facebook.com/franticassembly
Registered charity: 1113716

.

**STATE
THEATRE
COMPANY**
SOUTH AUSTRALIA

State Theatre Company South Australia is one of Australia's leading theatre companies performing an annual season of new Australian writing, reimagined classics and exceptional international writing in its home city of Adelaide. The Company is committed to the nurturing of Australian playwrights and to the development of South Australian theatre-makers.

The Company is currently led by Artistic Director Geordie Brookman, who has directed productions throughout Australia and Asia with his productions having Helpmann, Greenroom, Sydney Critics Circle, Adelaide Critics Circle and Curtain Call Awards.

State Theatre Company is a major community and cultural resource for all South Australians and is vital to artistic life in the state. Throughout its forty-five-year history, the Company has played a pivotal role in the careers of many of Australia's leading actors, writers and directors, attracting artists like Nathan Page, Miriam Margolyes, Xavier Samuel, Neil Armfield, Ruth Cracknell, Judy Davis, Gale Edwards, Mel Gibson, Garry McDonald, Geoffrey Rush, Jim Sharman, Hugo Weaving, Jacki Weaver and John Wood.

www.statetheatrecompany.com.au

Warwick Arts Centre in Coventry is an award-winning, multi-artform venue, it inspires people through the arts, culture, entertainment and learning.

One of the largest arts venues in the UK, Warwick Arts Centre opened in 1974 and welcomes over a million visitors every year. It makes meaningful, life-long connections with the local community and is a distinctive voice in the national and international arts world.

Situated on the campus of the University of Warwick, its work enhances the exceptional learning experience at the University and supports its strategic vision. With a high-quality programme of scale and impact, Warwick Arts Centre is an open-minded, ambitious and dedicated advocate of all art forms.

www.warwickartscentre.co.uk

Director   Alan Rivett
Programme Director   Julia Carruthers

CHICHESTER FESTIVAL THEATRE

Chichester Festival Theatre is one of the UK's flagship theatres with an international reputation for producing work of the highest quality, ranging from large-scale musicals to distinguished dramas. Situated in a cathedral city in West Sussex between the South Downs and the sea, the Festival Theatre's bold thrust stage design makes it one of England's most striking playhouses; a studio theatre, the Minerva Theatre, sits nearby.

The newly refurbished Festival Theatre reopened in 2014, following the completion of a major project to restore and upgrade its Grade II* listed building. With a transformed auditorium, increased seating capacity, more spacious foyer areas with new cafés, bars and outdoor terraces, as well as improved and expanded artist facilities, Chichester Festival Theatre has proudly matched its world-class artistic reputation with world-class spaces.

Numerous Chichester productions are being presented in London this year. Jonathan Kent's staging of *Young Chekhov* transferred to the National Theatre and Michael Morpurgo's *Running Wild* received its London premiere at Regent's Park Open Air Theatre. *Guys and Dolls* played at the West End's Savoy and Phoenix Theatres while simultaneously touring the UK. Following its run in Chichester this autumn, the National Theatre and Chichester Festival Theatre production of James Graham's *This House* will transfer to the Garrick Theatre in November; and *Love's Labour's Lost* and *Much Ado About Nothing* will transfer to the West End from December, jointly presented by the Royal Shakespeare Company, CFT and the Theatre Royal Haymarket.

Alongside its productions, the Theatre has a much-valued programme of learning and participation work. It has built and strengthened connections within the community through Youth Theatre groups, classes in writing, dance, and drama for a variety of ages, and Heritage activities to document its rich history.

www.cft.org.uk

Chairman   Sir William Castell
Artistic Director   Daniel Evans
Executive Director   Rachel Tackley

The Lyric Hammersmith is one of the UK's leading producing theatres. For more than a hundred and twenty years it has been responsible for creating some of the UK's most adventurous and acclaimed theatrical work. It has also gained a national reputation for its work with and for children and young people and creates pathways into the arts for young talent from all backgrounds, helping to diversify our industry. Recent productions include our critically acclaimed annual pantomimes, the smash hit *Bugsy Malone*, the international tour and co-production with Filter Theatre of *A Midsummer Night's Dream* and the UK premiere of the international phenomenon *Terror*.

The Lyric's dual commitment to producing the highest quality contemporary theatre, whilst nurturing the creativity of young people is what makes it unique within the cultural ecology of the UK. It is a local theatre rooted in its community with a national and international reputation for the quality and innovation of its artistic work.

In April 2015 the Lyric reopened following a multi-million-pound capital project, which saw the addition of the Reuben Foundation Wing housing state-of-the-art facilities for theatre, dance, film, music, digital and more. The 'new' Lyric is now the largest creative hub in West London and home to an innovative partnership of like-minded leading arts organisations who work together to deliver life-changing creative opportunities for thousands of young West Londoners.

For more information, please visit **lyric.co.uk**

Artistic Director   Sean Holmes
Executive Director   Sian Alexander

Registered Charity, No. 278518

PREMIERE

Things I Know To Be True premiered at the Dunstan Playhouse, Adelaide Festival Centre, Adelaide in May 2016.

CAST

Pip Price	Georgia Adamson
Bob Price	Paul Blackwell
Rosie Price	Tilda Cobham-Hervey
Fran Price	Eugenia Fragos
Ben Price	Nathan O'Keefe
Mark Price	Tim Walter
Stage Manager	Melanie Selwood
Assistant Stage Manager	Alex Hayley

The play received its UK premiere at the Lyric Hammersmith, London, on 10 September 2016.

CAST

Mark Price	Matthew Barker
Pip Price	Natalie Casey
Ben Price	Richard Mylan
Rosie Price	Kirsty Oswald
Bob Price	Ewan Stewart
Fran Price	Imogen Stubbs
Directors	Geordie Brookman & Scott Graham
Set & Lighting Designer	Geoff Cobham
Costume Designer	Ailsa Paterson
Sound Designer	Andrew Howard
Casting Director	Sarah Hughes
Associate Director	Jonnie Riordan
Production Manager	Nick Ferguson
Acting Production Manager/ Technical Stage Manager	Nick Hill
Company Stage Manager	Fiona Kennedy
Deputy Stage Manager	Sarah Thomas
Production Lighting	Tom White
Production Sound	Rob Parkinson
Costume Supervisor	Laura Rushton

THINGS I KNOW TO BE TRUE

Andrew Bovell

Characters

THE PRICE FAMILY
BOB, *sixty-three, a retrenched auto factory worker*
FRAN, *fifty-seven, a senior nurse*

THEIR CHILDREN
PIP, *thirty-four, an education department bureaucrat*
MARK, *thirty-two, an IT specialist*
BEN, *twenty-eight, a financial services worker*

AND
ROSIE, *nineteen, who doesn't know who she is or what she
    wants to be yet*

Note on Text

A lack of punctuation at the end of a line indicates a sentence
shared by more than one character, and that the following line
should come straight in.

Setting

The play is set primarily in a suburban home in Hallett Cove, in
the southern suburbs of Adelaide, a provincial city in Australia.
It is not unlike any other working-class suburb in any
provisional city in the Western world.

A family room, a kitchen and patio extension at the back open
to a classic Australian backyard. A Hills Hoist, a lemon tree, a
well-cut lawn, a rose garden, a shed up the back somewhere and
an ancient eucalypt towering above.

The play takes place over a year.

It Begins Like This

BOB PRICE *stares at the telephone. His children are watching.*

PIP. It's late.

BEN. Past midnight.

PIP. And the phone starts to ring.

MARK. You're standing in your pyjamas and bare feet, still heavy with sleep because you've just been woken.

ROSIE. Your heart is beating.

BEN. Too fast.

ROSIE. Like it might go.

PIP. Any minute it might go.

ROSIE. And you know if you answer your life is going to change.

MARK. And you're not ready for it.

PIP. Even though you've been waiting for this call ever since we were old enough to stay out past nine.

BEN. Ever since you stopped tucking us in at night and turning off the light.

ROSIE. Ever since we came screaming into this world.

PIP. You've been waiting for this.

MARK. And you're thinking which one of my kids is in trouble?

ROSIE. Which one of my kids is hurt?

BEN. Which one of my kids is dead?

PIP. And how will I tell their mother?

BEN. You could turn around.

PIP. Walk away

ROSIE. Not answer.

MARK. But you know that this

BEN. Whatever this is

ROSIE. Just has to be faced.

The phone starts to ring… once… twice… three times… four times.

BOB *answers.*

BOB. Hello?

Berlin

ROSIE. Berlin. A winter coat. A travel bag. A red nose. And a broken heart.

I'm standing on the platform at the train station. It's cold. The train is late and my socks are wet. I'm not quite sure how I got here or where I'm meant to go next.

I met him four nights ago and he was the most beautiful boy I had ever seen. His name was Emmanuel, of course, and he came from Madrid.

I'd been travelling by myself for three months. The great European adventure. London. Dublin. Paris. Prague. Then Berlin. I'd been saving for a year. Café work, bar work, babysitting. Mum and Dad said don't go by yourself. It's too dangerous. Go on a tour or at least with some girlfriends.

I'll meet people. I told them. I'll be fine. But meeting people is harder than you think. I mean I did meet people, at hostels and stuff but mainly other Australians. And it was fun for a night or two. But the boys just wanted to have sex and I guess that's alright but if I wanted sex with an Australian boy I would have stayed in Hallett Cove.

So I go to the churches and the museums and the galleries and I walk through the cobbled streets and I sit in cafés trying to look mysterious and everything is so beautiful. Everything is what I was expecting it to be. And yet somehow I want it to be more.

I Skype home once a week and tell Mum and Dad what an amazing place Europe is. They've never been. I tell them I'm having the best time because I can't bear the thought of them being disappointed for me. And when I Skype my brother Mark, I pretend the camera on my iPad is broken because he knows me and he will see it in my face. He'll see that it's all a mess and he'll tell me to come home but I can't go home, not yet, I mean then, I couldn't go home then because it would be such a... defeat.

I don't know what it's meant to be. I don't know what I'm meant to do. I keep wondering when it will start. Life. When will life start?

And then there he is. At a club in Mitte. Dancing. With his shirt off. And I think, wow, that guy can really dance. That guy is like... fire. And then he looks over at me. Me? And I am gone. I pretend not to be. I try to be cool. To make it seem like I'm not interested. But I am so interested. And we dance until the sun comes up. And as we come out of the club into the light, I think this is it. This is life. I am living.

And I know he wants to take me home. To his place. Or to his friend's place. Or to someone's place, I'm not quite sure whose place it is, and I say okay. Because at last I am living and I don't want life to stop.

And when he kisses me I want to cry. Because I'd never been kissed like that. Not in Hallett Cove. And I'd never been kissed where he kissed me or touched quite like that. He seemed to know things and for once it didn't seem to matter that I didn't. Three days. Three days we stayed in bed. And after three days I knew some things too.

We don't even get up to eat. He disappears and comes back with a bowl of cereal and two spoons. And that's all we eat. Cereal. Out of the same bowl. For three days.

On the third night I watch him sleeping and I do that thing you shouldn't do. I think about the future. I imagine taking him home to meet Mum and Dad and my sister and brothers and and and how they will all love him, like they love me. And how clever I am and brave to have found such a man, such a beautiful man, different but the same and brought him all the way back to Hallett Cove and then, there I am... Oh, I am so embarrassed but suddenly there I am in our backyard with Dad's roses all around us and I'm walking across the lawn on his arm, and he's got tears in his eyes and Mum's there in a new dress, which she never lets herself have and my sister Pip is there with her husband Steve and their two girls. She got married in the backyard too. And Mark, my oldest brother who I adore is there with his girlfriend, Taylor. And then there's Ben, my other brother who's there with a girl who's new and won't last because they just don't with Ben and I love them all so much, sometimes I think too much, if you can love too much but now I have to make room for Emmanuel who's standing there in a suit and he is just so, so... so handsome... And I... I'm wearing a white dress... And I'm kind of surprised, kind of shocked because I never even knew that that's what I wanted. And maybe it's not what I want, it's what I think Mum and Dad will want for me but anyway I'm there in a white dress, on my father's arm, walking across the lawn and...

Then he wakes up and he looks at me as if he knows what I'm thinking and as if he wants to get up and run so I kiss him on his lips before he can. And he smiles. And I'm gone all over again. And we make love, so tenderly, so sweetly and after, as I drift off to sleep, lying on his chest, listening to the beat of his heart, thinking I could listen to this for the rest of my life, I think is this it, is this what falling in love is?

And when I wake up in the morning he's gone... along with four hundred euros from my wallet, my iPad, my camera, my favourite scarf and a large piece of my heart. I find a girl in the house, smoking a cigarette at the kitchen table and ask if she's seen him. She shrugs and says that he said something about going to see his girlfriend in London. She tells me to get my things and to get out of her house.

I walk through the streets of Berlin. I feel small. I feel like I'm twelve years old, I feel ridiculous. I want to cry but I won't. Well I do, a bit. But not as much as I want to. I want my dad. I want my mum. I want my brothers and my sister. I want to hear them laugh and argue and fight and tease me. But I can't think of them much because if I do my chest will explode. I feel like I'm going to literally fall to pieces. That my arms are going to drop off and then my legs and my head. And so to stop myself coming apart I make a list of all the things I know... I mean actually know for certain to be true and the really frightening thing is... It's a very short list.

I don't know much at all.

But I know that at 25 Windarie Avenue, Hallett Cove, things are the same as when I left and they always will be.

And I know that I have to go home.

Home

The roses are in bloom. BOB *is using the leaf blower. He blows
this way. He blows that way. He hasn't quite got the hang of it.*

FRAN *appears at the back door. She wears a nurse's uniform.*

FRAN. Bob... Bob... BOB!

> *He blows her.*

> Stop it!

> *He blows her again. She raises a warning finger at him.
> She's not in the mood.*

> The kids have to be picked up at three fifteen.

BOB. I know.

FRAN. But you can't be late.

BOB. I'm never late.

FRAN. You were late on Monday.

BOB. Five minutes. That's not late.

FRAN. It takes two minutes to grab a child and put her in
your car.

BOB. You know that, do you?

FRAN. There's dinner in the fridge. Some bolognese. Just heat
it in the microwave. Pip will pick them up at six.

BOB. I'm going to see about getting rid of that tree.

FRAN. You're not touching that tree.

BOB. It makes a mess of the garden.

FRAN. Good. Give you something to do.

BOB. It's going to drop a bough one day, right on the shed.

FRAN. With you in it if I'm lucky.

BOB. It's a bloody eyesore.

FRAN. It's the most beautiful thing in the garden. It's the only
    thing that doesn't grow in a straight line and hasn't been
    pruned to within an inch of its life.

She turns to go inside. ROSIE *is standing there, wearing her
winter coat with her backpack over her shoulder like she'd
never been away.*

ROSIE. Hi.

FRAN. Where the hell did you come from?

ROSIE. Berlin.

BOB. Rosie!

ROSIE. I'm home.

FRAN. What's happened? What's wrong with you?

ROSIE. Nothing.

FRAN. Bob?

BOB. Are you hurt?

ROSIE. No.

FRAN. Sick?

ROSIE. I'm fine.

*Somewhere in here, amongst the talk and all the questions,
there are hugs and kisses.*

BOB. When did you get in?

ROSIE. About an hour ago. It took me a while to get through
    customs.

FRAN*'s already dialling her phone.*

BOB. Why didn't you call?

ROSIE. I wanted to surprise you.

BOB. I would have picked you up… I would have been there.

ROSIE. I caught a taxi.

BOB. Well, how much did that cost?

FRAN (*on phone*). It's me.

BOB. Fran?

FRAN (*phone*). Rosie's back.

BOB. She caught a taxi.

FRAN (*phone*). Something's happened.

ROSIE. Mum!

BOB. Did he come the coast road at least?

ROSIE. It was a she and she came down the expressway.

FRAN (*phone*). I think you should come over.

ROSIE. It didn't really matter. There wasn't much traffic.

BOB. Well, that's it, Rosie. They think the expressway is quicker but if there's no traffic it's better to take the coast road.

FRAN. That was Pip. She's on her way.

BOB. You should have called.

FRAN. I'll call your brothers.

BOB. Look at you.

ROSIE. I know.

BOB. Frannie.

FRAN. I know. (*Then back to the phone*.) It's Mum. Rosie's just walked in… I know but she's here. Something's happened.

ROSIE. Mum!

BOB. You look…

ROSIE. Different?

BOB. No.

ROSIE. All grown up?

BOB. Just the same.

FRAN. Mark's on his way.

ROSIE. I'm meant to look older, Dad.

BOB. Well, you haven't been away that long, love.

FRAN (*phone*). Ben… Rosie's back.

ROSIE. I wanted to surprise you.

BOB. You did.

FRAN (*phone*). Something's happened.

ROSIE. Mum!

FRAN. He's on his way.

ROSIE. Nothing's happened.

FRAN. Look at you.

ROSIE. I know.

FRAN. You look…

ROSIE. Just the same.

FRAN. No. You look…

ROSIE. What?

FRAN. Did you meet someone?

ROSIE. No.

FRAN. A boy?

ROSIE. No.

FRAN. Did he hurt you?

BOB. Who hurt you?

FRAN. A boy.

ROSIE. Mum, I've just walked in the door. You have to stop asking questions because I don't have the answers. Not now. Not yet. And if you keep asking I'm going to cry. I'm home. Okay? That's as much as I know right now.

FRAN. Okay. You're home… Bob… She's home.

BOB. I know.

FRAN. We can sleep again.

PIP *enters*.

PIP. Rosie!

ROSIE. Hi.

Embraces. Kisses.

PIP. Look at you.

FRAN. I know. She's here. Can you believe it?

BOB. Just walks in through the front door. Not even a phone call. And she catches a taxi... Pip? From the airport.

PIP. What for?

BOB. Exactly! When there're all these cars here. And people to pick her up. What's the point of a family if they can't pick you up at the airport?

ROSIE. I wanted to surprise you.

BOB. I'm still getting up off the floor, love.

PIP. You look...

ROSIE. Exactly the same, apparently.

PIP. What's happened?

ROSIE. Nothing.

PIP. Mum said...

ROSIE. I know but...

PIP. Why have you come back early?

FRAN. Somebody hurt her.

ROSIE. Mum!

FRAN. A boy.

PIP. Oh, Rosie. Really?

ROSIE. No!

PIP. Are you okay?

ROSIE. I don't want this to be about that. (*Appealing to* BOB.) Dad?

BOB. Now... now, she's right. Give the girl some air. She's not ready to talk about it.

BEN (*entering*). Rosie... what happened?

PIP. A guy hurt her.

BEN. What's his name... where is he?

They embrace.

Hey, little sister. I've missed you. Where have you been again? Hey, Mr Nap-a-Lot.

BOB. She caught a taxi.

BEN. From the airport?

BOB. Of all the things.

BEN. I would have picked you up.

BOB. That's what I said.

BEN. You should have called.

BOB. I told her.

BEN. I'm making coffee. Who wants coffee?

PIP. I can't stay.

FRAN. You can stay for a moment.

PIP. I'm late, Mum.

FRAN. But Rosie's here.

ROSIE. Where's Steve and the girls?

PIP. At home. They've got school.

FRAN. Dad's picking them up at three fifteen. Go with him. Make sure he's not late.

BOB. I'm never late.

PIP. You were late on Monday.

BOB. Pip's been promoted.

ROSIE. Really... that's fantastic.

PIP. I'm starting so early and finishing later.

BOB. She's running the whole department... a whole
government department.

PIP. No, I'm not.

BOB. It's incredible what she does.

PIP. I'm overseeing curriculum development. It's temporary.
I'm filling in for someone.

BOB. She's reporting directly to the Minister for Education.

PIP. Just to his advisers, actually.

BOB. But you've met the Minister.

PIP. Once.

BOB. Well, there you go. They even sent her overseas.

ROSIE. Where?

PIP. Vancouver. It was just a conference.

FRAN. She's lucky she's got help.

PIP. I know that, Mum.

FRAN. I'm just saying with Steve. He's good with the kids.

PIP. Yeah, he's great. He's their dad.

FRAN. With a job of his own.

PIP. That's right... He's a father and he's got an important job
of his own. He's amazing.

FRAN. I'm just saying that some men can't manage it as well
as he does.

PIP. I know that. I don't need you to tell me.

FRAN. Well, excuse me for having an opinion on the matter.

PIP. Can I scream now? Would anyone mind if I screamed now?

BEN. This hasn't been used... Dad, why haven't you used this?

FRAN. He hasn't worked it out, yet.

BEN. But I showed him. Dad, I showed you. You stick in a pod
and turn it on. I don't understand why you don't use the
things I give you.

FRAN. He does.

BOB. Because I don't need them, son. I don't need coffee machines and leaf blowers when a rake does the job just as well and I drink tea. Sometimes, I think you've got more money than sense.

BEN. Well, I work for it.

BOB. You want to put a little away. That's all I'm saying.

FRAN. I'll have a coffee. Rosie, you want coffee? Pip?

PIP. I have to go.

FRAN. Make your sisters a coffee, Ben. I'll have a latte. (*Aside to* BOB.) Give him a break.

MARK (*entering*). Rosie.

She moves to him and they embrace – a moment.

I thought you'd got away.

ROSIE. So did I.

BEN. You want coffee, Mark?

MARK. I can't stay.

FRAN. You just walked in.

BOB. Why don't you make me one of those after all, son.

FRAN. Show him how to do it, Ben. It's good to learn new things, Bob.

BOB. Yeah, give me a look at that thing.

MARK. What happened over there?

ROSIE. I don't want to talk about it.

MARK. Okay.

ROSIE. How's Taylor?

An elephant walks into the room.

FRAN. He didn't tell you?

MARK. We split up.

ROSIE. Really?

FRAN. A month ago.

ROSIE. Are you okay?

MARK. I'm working on it.

FRAN. She left him.

MARK. It was mutual.

FRAN. Packed a bag and walked out without an explanation.

MARK. Were you there, Mum?

FRAN. And why wouldn't she?

MARK. You don't know what happened.

FRAN. I've got a pretty good idea.

MARK. No, actually you don't.

FRAN. She wanted children.

MARK. Did she?

FRAN. And you wouldn't be in it.

MARK. Is that right?

FRAN. Then what? Tell me. A woman just doesn't walk away
    like that.

BOB. Now... now, come on. We won't have any of that. Rosie
    has just got home.

FRAN. Look, I liked her. She was a part of this family for three
    years. And then one day she's gone and you give us nothing.
    We're not even allowed to say goodbye. I miss her. I thought
    she was the one. I'd made room for her.

MARK. I know, Mum.

ROSIE (*to* MARK). I'm sorry.

BEN. I've got to get going.

FRAN. We'll have dinner tonight. All together. Bob, pick up
    a few chickens from the butcher when you get the kids.

BEN. Mum, I've got plans.

FRAN. What do you mean? Rosie's home. Change them. And don't forget to take your washing. It's folded up on your bed.

PIP. You still do his washing?

FRAN. Only on Sundays.

BEN. It's just my shirts.

PIP. Mum!

FRAN. He does his own underwear.

PIP. You're not doing him any favours.

FRAN. He works in an office. He has to look smart.

PIP. So? He can learn how to iron. He's twenty-eight.

BEN. Mum helps you with the kids.

PIP. So?

BEN. I'm just saying.

PIP. That's different.

BEN. Why?

PIP. Because she'll help you with your kids too. If you ever find a woman stupid enough to have them with.

FRAN. Don't say that. Of course he will. What kind of thing is that to say?

PIP. I just said, Mum, you're not doing him any favours.

FRAN. It's my washing machine. It's my house. He's my son. I'll wash his clothes if I want to.

BOB. This coffee's not bad.

PIP (to MARK). Will you back me up?

MARK. Ben, wash your own clothes.

BEN. I do! It's just my shirts. I can't get them like she does.

PIP. Then take them to a laundry and pay for it.

FRAN. What's the matter, Pip? You think you're missing out on something here?

PIP. You work, Mum. You always have. You work harder and more hours than anyone in this family. You should not still be washing and ironing his shirts.

FRAN. That's my business.

PIP. I'm trying to defend you.

FRAN. I don't need defending from my own son.

PIP. I'm going.

MARK. Me too.

FRAN. No one misses out here. You understand? What one gets another one gets in a different way.

BOB. Who'd have thought it?

FRAN. What?

BOB. That she's been all over the world and now she's back. Our little Rosie. She was never meant to be here, you know. We thought we'd finished at the three kids.

MARK. That's my exit cue.

BOB. But South's were in the grand final.

PIP. And that's mine.

BOB. So it was a big night.

FRAN. Enough of that old story. We've all heard it too many times. It's enough to say that your father is lazy and irresponsible and should have had it on when he didn't.

BEN. Mum!

FRAN. And he was altogether too quick with his business anyway… so there was no joy in it for anyone but him but that's what will happen on grand final night after a few beers and let that be a warning to you all.

BOB. She's right, all of it's true but thank God for a little recklessness. Because look what came of it.

A moment as they all look upon ROSIE – *there's no question – they adore her, all of them. But life goes on as*

There's a flurry of kisses and goodbyes as car keys and mobile phones are gathered. This is a family that always kisses on greeting and parting. It is just second nature. The boys kiss their father as naturally as they kiss their mother.

FRAN. Don't forget the chickens, Rosie?

BEN. Has anyone seen my phone?

ROSIE. You want me to get them ready?

FRAN. I'll call you. Tell you how I want it done.

ROSIE. I know how to prepare a chicken.

FRAN. You don't know everything.

ROSIE. I probably do about this.

FRAN (*going*). You have to rub salt on the inside.

ROSIE. I know that.

BEN. Did someone put my phone somewhere?

PIP. You're so gorgeous. You know that?

ROSIE. I can't wait to see the kids. I've got presents for them.

PIP (*going*). You didn't have to do that.

ROSIE. Of course I did, I wanted to.

BEN. It's okay… it's here, I've got it. Thank you everyone for your concern.

MARK. I'll call you.

ROSIE. Are you okay?

MARK. I'm fine. I'm just really tired of answering that question. I'm sorry… I wish…

ROSIE. What?

MARK. That you'd got away.

ROSIE. I wasn't ready.

MARK (*going*). Don't leave it too long. You'll miss the chance. Like the rest of us.

BEN. Shit... I'm so late. (*Kissing* ROSIE, *going*.) I might not make it tonight. But don't tell Mum. Love you.

ROSIE. Ben... come. It will be good for us all to be together.

And suddenly everyone has gone and she is alone.

Somewhere in the flurry of the departures, BOB *has wandered into the garden and is dead-heading the spent roses.* ROSIE *joins him.*

BOB. Are you hungry?

ROSIE. I ate on the plane.

BOB. There's bolognese in the fridge.

ROSIE. I'm not eating much meat at the moment.

BOB. Well, there's probably cucumbers or something.

ROSIE. The roses look good.

BOB. They're still in their first flush, Rosie. They're at their best. Just like you.

ROSIE bends and smells a rose.

Are you going to tell me what happened over there?

ROSIE. I fell in love with the wrong guy.

BOB. Did it hurt?

ROSIE. So much, Dad.

BOB. Ah... well. I'll tell you something for free. Everyone has their heart broken, at least once. Hopefully, for you it will be the only time.

ROSIE. Have you?

BOB. I've been with your mother since I was a kid. First and only love.

A moment – ROSIE breathes, safe in the certainty of her parents' love and in the familiar surrounds of her father's garden. For a moment everything is right, everything is as it should be.

ROSIE. All those cities. All those beautiful cities. All that history. All through Europe. And all I could think about was coming home.

BOB. It's not such a bad place.

ROSIE. I tried, Dad.

BOB. To do what, love?

ROSIE. To grow up.

Autumn

Pip

It's early in the morning. The light is still new. Leaves drift from trees. Fallen rose petals form a carpet of bruised colour across the lawn.

PIP *is sitting in the garden.*

PIP. This garden is the world. Everything that matters happened here.

I kissed my first boy in that shed. I was nine. He was my cousin, Tom. Down from Port Augusta. I don't know if it counts if it was your cousin. But it was a kiss, nonetheless. He kissed me and then he put his hand down my pants. I don't know what he expected but I think he got a shock because he pulled it straight back out again. But I liked it. I got so excited that I bit his face. He started to cry and ran to his mother and I was sent to my room. And I don't know if it was because I bit him or because I liked having his hand down my pants. Somehow, I think Mum knew. I think she knew exactly why a girl bites a boy in the face. But then she always knew the things you didn't want her to know.

She caught us, me and Penny McCrea and Stella Bouzakis with a bottle of sweet wine. We were in Year 9 and we snuck off from school at lunchtime. Penny had stolen it from her parents' drinks cabinet. We came back here and made a party of it, smoking those long coloured cocktail cigarettes as well. Thinking we were totally it. And suddenly Mum's standing at the back door. She was meant to be at work. She never came home for lunch. Never. But that day, when we're wagging school and drinking sweet wine in the backyard she decides to come home. Stella got such a scare she started to vomit. Mum stuck her face in the compost pit and said 'Vomit there, you silly girl'. I was grounded for the rest of Year 9 and never drank sweet wine again.

This garden is the world.

Family cricket and totem tennis tournaments. Hey Presto!
and cartwheels across the lawn. Fashion parades and
sleepovers. Sunday barbecues. Eighteenth birthday parties.
Twenty-firsts. Engagements. And even a wedding. Mine.
It all happened here and more.

Once I saw her, Mum, bawling her eyes out and banging her
head against the trunk of that tree. I was twelve. I had never
seen her cry. Not once. Not even when her own mother died.
And everything I thought was certain about the world
changed. I went back inside and turned the television on. I was
scared. What makes a woman cry like that? A mother. My
mother. I didn't understand and I didn't have the courage to
ask her. Now, that I am a woman, married with children of my
own I don't need to, I know exactly why a woman bashes her
head against the trunk of a tree.

*She hums a few bars from a Leonard Cohen song: 'Famous
Blue Raincoat.'*

(*Sings.*)
    It's four in the morning, the end of December
    I'm writing to you now, just to see if you're better

She becomes quiet.

This garden was the world.

FRAN *is watching. She is dressed for work… as always.*
ROSIE *joins her having just risen from bed.*

ROSIE (*seeing* PIP). What's wrong?

FRAN. Get a blanket… The quilt from her bed. The one that
she knows. And Rosie… wake your dad.

ROSIE *moves off as* FRAN *moves outside to join* PIP.

You're up with the birds.

PIP. I've been for a jog.

FRAN. What's going on?

PIP. Can't I visit and sit for a moment in the garden where
I grew up.

FRAN. Is that what you call it now, when you come? A visit?
A visit is something a relative you don't know very well does
once a year. Something you've just got to get through. This
is different. This is you, coming home, which you do three or
four times a week. The thing is when you come you don't sit.
You come. You do what needs to be done and then you go.
That's the way it is. So now I find you sitting and I'm pretty
sure something is wrong.

BOB *emerges from the house doing up his dressing gown.*

BOB. What's going on?

FRAN. Pip is visiting.

BOB. What's wrong?

FRAN. There you go… Why don't you make some coffee, Bob?

BOB. Well, I would if I knew how to work that machine.

FRAN. Rosie will show you.

BOB. You want milk, Pip?

PIP. Black thanks, Dad.

BOB. Visiting?

BOB *goes back inside.*

FRAN. Is this about Steve?

PIP. I'm leaving him.

FRAN. Does he know yet?

PIP. He will soon.

FRAN. You might want to drop the kids over. Give yourselves
some room to talk.

PIP. You're not surprised?

FRAN. No. I could see this coming. The writing's been on the
wall for some time.

PIP. What did it say, Mum? This writing.

FRAN. It said 'I'm not happy'. In big black letters.

PIP. Don't.

FRAN. What?

PIP. Make out like you know more about my life than I do.

FRAN. I'm just saying.

PIP. Let me be the expert on that at least.

FRAN. Somebody got up on the wrong side of bed this morning.

PIP. This was a bad idea.

She rises to go.

FRAN. Don't you walk away from this… You're not twelve years old any more.

PIP. What will you do, Mum? Pull my hair? Slap my face?

ROSIE *has come out of the house with the quilt. She has caught the last of the exchange. She wraps the quilt around* PIP's *shoulders.* PIP *takes it in, and is grateful for its comfort.*

ROSIE. Dad's made a mess of the coffee so we're having tea.

PIP. Rosie, do you remember when you fell off the ladder?

ROSIE. Not really, I was only two, wasn't I?

FRAN. Eighteen months. If that.

PIP. Mum asked me to watch you. She was busy inside.

FRAN. I was doing the house.

PIP. But I didn't really want to. I was trying to get a tan. I was lying in the sun in my bikini and Mum kept saying I would burn.

FRAN. You didn't have the skin for it. You still don't.

PIP. But I was determined that I'd have a tan that summer.

FRAN. You've got your father's skin.

PIP. I only closed my eyes for a moment. Dad had left the ladder up against the shed.

FRAN. He never did that again.

PIP. And I didn't know you could climb. Babies can't climb ladders.

FRAN. She could.

PIP. I can still hear the crack of your skull hitting the path.

FRAN. I heard it from the kitchen.

PIP. I screamed. Mum ran out of the house and saw what had happened. She looked at me and I swear I went cold. She could do that with just a look.

FRAN. I still can.

PIP. But particularly to me, Mum. You do that to me.

Beat.

I ran into the house and hid under the bed. And she came after me.

FRAN. Here we go.

PIP. You came after me and pulled me out from under the bed by my hair.

FRAN. Well, you wouldn't come out.

PIP. By my hair.

FRAN. I couldn't reach anything else.

PIP. You tore the hair from my head.

FRAN. It was just a few strands.

PIP. It was a clump with skin. And then you slapped my face.

FRAN. I was in shock. I was angry. I was tired. Four kids I had and one day a week to clean the house. And I asked you to do one thing. To watch over your sister. But you were too selfish. And too vain to do it.

PIP. Vain?

FRAN. Lying in the sun like you were Princess Bloody Muck instead of watching your sister.

ROSIE. Dad… How's the tea going?

PIP. I wasn't vain. I was just trying to fit in. To be like all the other girls.

ROSIE. I'll see how he's going.

PIP. Stay… Rosie. Would you?… I was a mouse. A mouse, Mum. The only thing I thought was pretty about me was my hair. Which is what you tore out of my head. Funny that.

FRAN. It was a moment. A moment of anger.

PIP. I had a bald patch for a whole term. It still doesn't grow properly there.

FRAN. It was one time. And now what? You're unhappy because I pulled your hair when you were twelve years old.

PIP. I was fourteen.

BOB *comes into the garden with the tea tray.*

FRAN. Are you going to tell him or will I?

PIP. Go right ahead.

FRAN. She's leaving Steve.

BOB. Steve?

FRAN. Well, who else would she be leaving, Bob?

BOB. Why?

FRAN. Because I pulled her hair when she was fourteen years old and she's been unhappy ever since.

ROSIE. Mum!

BOB. Pip?

PIP. It hasn't been good for a while, Dad.

BOB. Well, I know there's been a rough patch. But that's true for most marriages.

PIP. I've tried.

BOB. Well, have you thought about trying some more?

PIP. I'm not happy, Dad.

FRAN. There's that word, Bob. Happy. As if that is the point of living.

BOB. And what about Steve? How's he feel about it?

PIP. I think he'd like things to stay the same.

FRAN. You have a husband who loves you, who treats you well, who's a wonderful father and you're walking away from that.

PIP. Not easily.

FRAN. It doesn't make sense.

PIP. I know. He's a good man.

FRAN. Oh, I get it.

PIP. What?

FRAN. There's someone else?

PIP. No.

FRAN. Look at me.

PIP. I'm doing this for myself.

FRAN. Yeah, that much is clear.

PIP. Can you just take my side, Mum?

FRAN. The man's done nothing wrong. He's loved you and been a good father. Why would I make an enemy of him?

PIP. I don't love him.

FRAN. Too bad. You've got kids. You make it work. Look at me and tell me there's no other man.

She looks at her... FRAN *thinks she sees the lie in her face.*

You stupid girl!

PIP. Don't.

FRAN. Why would you do that to yourself?

BOB. She said there's no one.

FRAN. Please, God, tell me he's not married.

ROSIE. Mum... Please don't.

BOB. What about the girls... where are they in all this?

PIP. I've been offered a position in Vancouver. I'm going to take it.

FRAN. You're taking the girls from him too?

PIP. They're staying here.

FRAN (*to* BOB). Do you hear that?

BOB. Now hold on... I don't think that's right, Pip.

PIP. The position is for twelve months... I'm going to see how it goes. At the end we'll decide what's best.

FRAN. Do you hear what she's saying?

PIP. If it was a man making this decision... If it was Mark or Ben you would support it. There would be no question that they should do this.

FRAN. Not if they were walking out on their kids.

PIP. My work is important to me, Mum. This is a professional opportunity. I'm going to take it.

FRAN. And who's going to pick up the slack with the kids? I've been a mother for thirty-four years. I'm over it.

PIP. I'm not asking you to do anything more than you already do.

FRAN. How's he going to manage for twelve months? On his own.

PIP. The same as I would if it was him that was going.

FRAN. But you'd have me. And Dad. You know you would. Day and night. And you've gone ahead on this knowing we will be there.

ROSIE. I'll be able to help.

FRAN. Shut it, Rosie.

ROSIE. I'm just saying I would help.

FRAN. You made a choice. Nine years ago. To have children. You don't walk away from that.

PIP. Things don't have to stay the same... people work these things out differently now. Steve is as good a parent as I am.

FRAN. Those girls need their mother.

PIP. Not if she is unhappy.

FRAN. You selfish bitch.

BOB. Jesus, Fran.

FRAN. Your happiness is not what matters here.

BOB. Pull it back a notch would you?

PIP. Because you know what happens then, Mum? She will
make sure her children are unhappy too. She will choose one
and she will make sure that she feels like shit about herself.

FRAN. What happened, Pip? Did some guy bored with his wife
look twice at you and make you feel like you were more than
a mouse?

BOB. What's the matter with you?

FRAN. She's walking out on her kids. What's the matter with
you? Christ, Bob. You know what you get when you treat a
girl like a princess. You get a fucking princess.

BOB. Oh, we're swearing now, are we?

PIP. You're going to annihilate me.

FRAN. Toughen up… You'll need to if you're planning to
shack up with some Canadian for the winter.

BOB. Stop it!

FRAN. Or what? You'll raise your hand to me. You'll do it once
and once only, Bob Price.

FRAN *walks inside – a moment*.

BOB (*to* ROSIE). Go and see if your mother's all right… I want
a moment with Pip.

ROSIE *goes inside*.

Is she right? Is there something more to this? Someone else?

A moment… He couldn't bear it to be true.

PIP. No.

BOB. All right then… You're an intelligent woman. You know your own mind. If this is an opportunity then grab it with both hands. Because life is horribly short. And there's no gain staying with a man who you have no love for, no matter how good a man he is. You'll just end up hurting him. Or hurting him more than you already have. I'll come on board with the kids, you know that. And so will your mum. Once things have settled down.

PIP embraces her father.

Treat Steve with respect now… I'm fond of him.

PIP. So am I, Dad… That's the problem.

BOB. What do you mean?

PIP. A woman needs to feel more than fondness for her husband.

She leaves. BOB *takes a moment before* FRAN *joins him from inside.*

FRAN. Daddy make everything all right again, did he?

BOB. Here we go.

FRAN. She's lying.

BOB. There's one thing I ask of my kids. One thing! Absolute honesty. She knows that a lie to my face would kill me.

Beat.

You want to try listening for a change. Just listening to the girl instead of always thinking that you're right… And I would never strike you.

They hold on each other for an unforgiving moment until she gives a little ground.

FRAN. I know that.

She picks up the quilt where it has dropped in the fray. She folds it and holds it close to her chest.

As Autumn Turns

The branches are bare and the rose bushes are pruned back for the winter. BOB *is spreading manure on the beds.*

FRAN *and* ROSIE *work side by side in the kitchen.* ROSIE *is cutting onions.*

FRAN. What are you going to do with yourself?

ROSIE. Mum, not this conversation, please.

FRAN. One gap year's all very well. Two is starting to look like a girl who doesn't know herself very well... You should think about nursing. It's honest work and decent money.

ROSIE. I'm just not ready to decide.

FRAN. What's the most important thing in a woman's life? And don't make the mistake of thinking it's love.

ROSIE. I wasn't. (*She was.*)

FRAN. Or children. Those things are fine but they are not what matter. It's independence. Without that the others are just a trap. A woman needs to stand on her own feet and earn her own money. That's the best advice you'll ever get from me. So get a job.

ROSIE. I've got a job.

FRAN. One that you'll still want to be doing when you're forty years old and not so pretty.

ROSIE. You always make me cut the onions. You say, come, I'll teach you to cook but I only end up cutting onions.

FRAN. And look how well you cut them.

ROSIE. It's not fair.

FRAN. It's a mother's job to make her children cry... one way or another.

ROSIE. Why?

FRAN. So they understand pain.

ROSIE. That is so wrong.

At some point BOB *has stopped as if he has forgotten what to do next.*

FRAN. What's he doing?

ROSIE. I don't know.

FRAN. Bob!

ROSIE. Sssh.

FRAN. BOB!

BOB *looks up.*

What are you doing?

BOB. What?

FRAN. The manure. You're doing the garden.

BOB. I know.

He wanders off.

FRAN. I'm not looking after him if he gets dementia. I've looked after people all my life.

ROSIE. Then I will.

FRAN. That's enough onion… Do me some carrots as well. A fine dice. Cubes. Not rectangles. (*Glances back out to the garden.*) I worry about him, Rosie.

ROSIE. He's all right… isn't he?

FRAN. I want to take him away.

ROSIE. Where to?

FRAN. To Europe. To America. To all those places you're meant to go. I want to leave you lot and all your troubles behind. I just want it to be him and me again. Before…

ROSIE. What?

FRAN. I forget what that's like.

ROSIE. Can you afford it?

FRAN. You're not to tell your dad but I've got a stash.

ROSIE. Of what?

FRAN. Of money. What do you think? I've always put a little away. Since my very first pay packet. Even if it was just five dollars. It adds up, Rosie. Compound interest!

BOB (*from the garden*). Fran…

FRAN. What?

BOB. Have you used my secateurs?

FRAN. No.

> BOB *wanders off not entirely convinced by her denial.*

> He's older than he needs to be. And he knows much less of the world than he should.

ROSIE. Yeah… but he's happy with what he has, Mum.

FRAN. That's because he thinks he doesn't deserve more. You work for a carmaker for thirty years. You know nothing else and then they close the doors and tell you you're not needed any more. They give you a package and tell you that's what you're worth. And it seems like a hell of a lot when it's given to you all at once, if all you know is a fortnightly pay packet and so you believe them. A few years later it's nearly all gone and you realise you weren't worth much at all. And so you satisfy yourself with a bed of roses… I hate those roses.

ROSIE. Mum!

FRAN. They're just an excuse for not living.

ROSIE. Why don't you stop work? So you've got more time together.

FRAN. Because I'd bash him to death with the back of a shovel if I had to spend all day with him and then I'd kill myself from boredom. No. I like work. I like who it lets me be.

> BEN *enters with his shirts.*

BEN. I can't stay.

FRAN. Are you hungry?

BEN. What is there?

FRAN. There's lasagne in the fridge.

BEN. Can I take it with me?

FRAN. Put it in a Tupperware. And make sure you bring it
    back. You've got all my containers over there, already.

BOB (*entering*). What's that parked in the drive?

BEN. I know… What do you think?

BOB. It's a little flash.

BEN. What do you mean?

BOB. It looks new.

BEN. It's off the floor… I got a deal.

BOB. It's European.

BEN. So?

BOB. What are you trying to prove?

BEN. I'm not trying to prove anything. That's just what people
    drive.

BOB. What people?

BEN. I don't know. People. People I know. People I work with.
    Jesus, it's just a car.

BOB. Did you get finance for it?

BEN. Yeah, what else?

BOB. You didn't want to talk that over with me, first?

BEN. What? You're a bank manager now?

FRAN. He can afford it… Can't you?

BOB. There was nothing wrong with the car you had.

FRAN. They're like that now, Bob. They don't drive the same
    car for long. Not the kind of people he's with.

BOB. What people? What people is he with? The kind of people who take out a seventy-grand loan to buy a new car, so that they can look better than they are?

BEN. Is that what you think?

FRAN. He's not saying that.

BOB. You're not even thirty years old and you're driving a brand-new car. European, no less.

BEN. I earn good money. Spending it is not a crime.

BOB. Your mum and I paid cash for our first new car. We saved for it. And you know what we did until we had enough in the bank?

BEN. Rosie... get me a pad and pencil. I should write this down and stick it on the fridge.

BOB. We lived with what we had... a second-hand bomb.

BEN. That was last century.

BOB. Nevertheless... we made do.

BEN. Yeah, well, I'm not prepared to work all my life for the same company for a handshake and a car at cost at the end of it. I want more than that.

BOB. It was cost and a bit more. They weren't so generous.

BEN. Well, there you go. You got screwed at the end anyway.

FRAN. Ben.

BOB. Are you insured?

BEN. Of course.

BOB. Full comprehensive?

BEN. I'm not an idiot.

BOB. Right then, it's in your hands.

    BOB *returns to the garden.*

BEN (*as he goes*). I'll take you for a spin... if you want.

    BOB *doesn't reply.*

ROSIE. You can take me.

BEN. Maybe next time, Rosie.

FRAN. You don't need to talk to him like that.

BEN. Like I said... I can't stay.

FRAN. You want to stand still... just for a moment, Ben. Just to take a look at what's going on around you.

BEN. Coming here is like a lesson in how to be a better person. I get it every time. I'm over it.

FRAN. Yeah, well that's our job.

He kisses her.

You want the lasagne?

BEN. No, Mum... I have to go.

BEN *exits.* FRAN *joins* BOB *in the garden.*

FRAN. He's doing well for himself... You might want to think about noticing that now and then.

BOB. He should have talked to me about it first.

FRAN. What would you have said?

BOB. I would have said don't do it.

FRAN. Well, there you go.

BOB. He doesn't think things through.

FRAN. He's young. Christ, Bob, it's a small window in which to shine and be foolish.

BOB. I wouldn't know about being young, Fran. I had two kids and a mortgage at his age.

FRAN. Yeah, well, you weren't there alone.

She goes back inside to ROSIE.

ROSIE. I'm thinking of moving out of home.

FRAN. And now's the time you choose to tell me?

ROSIE. I thought seeing how you're already upset.

FRAN. How will you pay your rent?

ROSIE. I'll get more hours.

FRAN. You won't go far. The youngest never does. You'll get a house around the corner.

ROSIE. I will not.

FRAN. It's better to buy than rent. We'll help you with the deposit. That way when the onions need cutting you won't have far to come.

ROSIE. You're trying to bribe me with a house?

FRAN. Why not? You're my favourite.

ROSIE. You can't say that.

FRAN. Don't worry. I tell you all the same thing.

ROSIE. Do you tell Pip?

FRAN. She's different.

ROSIE. Why?

FRAN. Because she's me… But stronger.

ROSIE. You should speak to her, Mum.

FRAN. I will… When she comes back and takes care of her kids like a normal woman.

ROSIE. I think she's happy.

FRAN. Well, good for her because nobody else is.

ROSIE. Anyway, it's not true I'm your favourite. Ben is.

FRAN. What can I say? The boy makes me laugh. He just has to walk into the room and I want to smile.

ROSIE. Mark's my favourite.

FRAN. Of course. He's loved you from the get go.

ROSIE. Why did Taylor leave?

FRAN. You'll have to ask him. He doesn't talk to me. Not about the important things.

BOB *enters holding a letter.*

BOB. The mail's come.

FRAN. So? It needs to be announced now?

BOB. There's a letter from Canada... It's addressed to you.

FRAN takes it and folds it into her uniform pocket before she moves outside. BOB and ROSIE are watching her expectantly from the house.

FRAN. I don't need an audience... Thank you very much.

ROSIE and BOB pretend to be busy as FRAN takes out the letter and opens it. She begins to read.

As PIP moves through the cycle of her day.

PIP. Dear Mum. It's cold in Vancouver but I like where I'm living. That's a reference to a Leonard Cohen song except he was talking about New York. But you know that, don't you. 'Famous Blue Raincoat'. You used to play it. Over and over.

(Sings.)
It's four in the morning, the end of December
I'm writing you now just to see if you're better
New York is cold but I like where I'm living
There's music on Clinton Street, all through the evening

I was on Skype with Katie the other day and I found myself thinking that she was a little plump. And wishing that her face was not quite so round and that her hair didn't fall quite so straight from her head. Is that what we do to our daughters? Praise them whilst we secretly think they're not good enough. The moment they start to become women, the first shedding of blood (do you remember how early I was?) and the first sign of a developing breast, is this when we start thinking that they're not pretty enough? Or smart enough? Is this when we start worrying that they're never going to find someone? Or be someone. Is this what we do? Maybe it's better that the girls are brought up by their father who looks at them and only sees the best. Like Dad. That's what Dad sees when he looks at me. I wish you could too.

(*Sings*.)
>   Yes, and Jane came by with a lock of your hair
>   She said that you gave it to her

FRAN *joins her on the third line*.

FRAN *and* PIP.
>   That night that you planned to go clear

FRAN *finishes alone*.

FRAN.
>   Did you ever go clear?

PIP. I never really understood the song when I was a girl. I still
don't. But I knew enough to know that it was about love and
that each time you played it you wanted to cry. You never did.
Not with us around. Only once did I see you let yourself go.
You thought you were alone. In the backyard. Leaning against
the old gum tree. Howling and howling. Bashing your head
against the trunk. Why were you crying that day, Mum?

FRAN *quickly wipes a tear away before it dares to fall*.

I'm sorry I never asked you. Why didn't we have those
conversations? I think that maybe we were too busy hiding
from each other the things that really mattered.

And so I'm sitting here in my apartment in Vancouver and
it's threatening to snow. And I hope that it does because
that's a good enough reason not to go out. And I'm playing
that song and wondering why it meant so much to you. And
I can only ask this from a distance because I'm scared of
seeing the truth in your face like you saw it in mine.

I met him at an education conference here in Vancouver on
that first trip. I didn't see it coming. Do you ever see it
coming? So yes, your accusation of another man was right.
Are you ever wrong, Mum?

I was ready. For him. For love. A Canadian. A public-
education specialist. A man who spoke with passion about
something that I'd stopped caring about years ago. It wasn't
hard. I was ready to fall. For someone. Someone who
reminded me of what mattered. And so I fell, Mum. In love.

Three days at a conference. Six months of thrilling emails and text messages and clandestine phone calls and I knew that I had to come.

He's married. Of course. You knew that too. Three children. A son and two daughters. To a woman who is good and fine and right and beautiful. But I don't care. Because I feel loved. By him. Like I have never felt loved by Steve. My good sweet husband who has done nothing but care for me and the children but who does not look much further in life than the end of his own driveway. And now, I'm waiting for his call, my lover, wondering if tonight he will find the excuse to leave his good wife, his sweet children and his safe home and come to me.

I didn't want to be this woman, Mum. But I can't leave. I won't. Eventually, he will have to make a choice and it probably won't be me. But for now... well, for now, I am this woman.

'Thanks for taking the trouble from her eyes'. Do you remember that line from the song? That is what this man has done for me. And I'm wondering if there was someone who could have done it for you, if you let them.

My love, Pip.

FRAN *sits in the silence of the garden.* BOB *has come out of the house and is watching.*

BOB. Is everything all right?

FRAN. It's fine.

BOB. What does she say?

FRAN. She says it's cold in Vancouver.

Winter

Mark

The roses are bare and the sky is grey. FRAN *is in the garden smoking a cigarette.*

MARK. On the weekends when Dad wanted help in the garden I would climb the gum tree and hide. From up there, I could see the world.

At least I could see our world. Pip singing to a song on the radio and checking her split ends at the patio table. Ben kicking the football from one end of the yard to the other. Always running. Dad pushing a wheelbarrow of dirt around with Rosie following him with her plastic shovel ready to help. And Mum hanging out the washing before sneaking a cheeky fag behind the shed, thinking that no one knows she's there.

They didn't know I was up in the tree watching and seeing everything. Not really a part of the picture and not really even knowing why.

There were two occasions on which Mum would smoke. The first was if she'd had more than two glasses of wine. She wasn't a big drinker so this was rare. It usually happened on New Year's Eve. She would light up after two glasses of sparkling wine and only ever smoke the one. She was also known to dance with Dad's undies on her head, after he had taken them off for God knows what reason, so New Year's Eve was always an ordeal for us kids. The other occasion was when she thought that one of us had a problem that she couldn't solve, which was also rare, Mum having a solution for most problems in life. And on these occasions she could go through a pack, one after another until a solution was found. I suspect that of all of us, she smoked the most cigarettes on account of me.

BOB *is pushing a load of dirt across the yard when he finds* FRAN.

BOB. What the hell are you doing?

FRAN. Sssh, I don't want Rosie to see.

BOB. Well, give me a puff?

FRAN. No. One puff for you and you'd be back on a pack a day. Mark called. He's coming over.

BOB. Good... I'll get him to help me shift the garden furniture. There's a storm coming in.

FRAN. He says he needs to talk to us.

BOB. What about?

FRAN. Now you're not to go on but I think he might be gay.

BOB. Bloody hell!

FRAN. See... there you go.

BOB. Well, it's a bit out of the blue!

FRAN. He doesn't know we know so you'll have to act surprised.

BOB. Well, I am. I mean why hasn't he told us before?

FRAN. It takes some men longer, that's all.

BOB. So this is why Taylor up and left, you think?

FRAN. I'd say so... Are you all right with it?

BOB. Yes... if he is. If it's the way he wants to go.

FRAN. It's not a way you go, Bob. It's not a direction you take.

BOB. I didn't mean that. I mean he's thirt... how old is he?

FRAN. Thirty-two.

BOB. Exactly! He's thirty-two. His life is his own.

FRAN. That's right.

BOB. And you? Are you all right with it?

FRAN. Yes!... I think so. I mean it's not what you think you're going to get when you have kids.

BOB. No.

FRAN. I mean a part of me thinks Not My Son. Please God not my son. Let it be some other woman's son. But apart from that, no, I'm fine with it.

BOB. Yeah, it sounds like it too.

They share a moment, a laugh.

Anyway, no matter what, he's still going to be our boy... It's starting to rain.

***

The storm breaks.

A little later that night. MARK*'s at the back door, wet from the rain.* BOB *and* FRAN *are fussing over him.*

FRAN. You're soaked through.

MARK. I walked over.

BOB. In this weather?

FRAN. Rosie, get a towel.

BOB. You'll catch your death.

MARK. It wasn't raining when I left.

BOB. Why didn't you take an umbrella?

MARK. I told you it wasn't raining.

BOB. It's the middle of winter, son. You go for a walk the chances are you're going to get wet.

FRAN *takes the towel from* ROSIE *and starts to dry* MARK*'s hair.*

MARK. I'll do it, Mum.

BOB. Take that shirt off. Rosie, get him a shirt from my drawer. What about your pants?

MARK. They're fine, thanks.

FRAN *is starting to take* MARK*'s shirt off.*

Mum!

FRAN. You think I haven't seen you naked before?

He removes his own shirt.

Would you look at the colour of him? When's the last time you saw any sun? That's your fault, Bob. White as a bloody ghost. Both of you. And have you had that mole checked out? I don't like the look of that.

ROSIE (*entering with shirt*). Is blue okay?

MARK. Right now polka dots would be fine.

He takes the shirt and puts it on.

BOB. So are you hungry?

MARK. I'm fine.

BOB. I could fix you something.

MARK. I've eaten.

FRAN. What exactly? Because you're as skinny as a rake.

BOB. There's your mum's stew in the fridge. I'll heat it up.

MARK. What's the matter with you two? I said I've eaten. I'm fine. And I'm not too skinny and I'm not too white. And I haven't got skin cancer. Can we have a conversation for once that doesn't begin with you making a list of everything that's wrong with me? And could you stand still for half a minute because I'm trying to tell you something here and it's not easy.

FRAN. Look, Mark, there's nothing you could tell us that would shock us or make us feel any different about you. I just want to say that.

BOB. Unless you told us you had decided to become a woman. Then I would be shocked.

BOB *laughs at his joke. He's the only one though. It's a terrible silence as they realise what's just been inelegantly revealed.*

MARK. That's not how this was meant to go.

They are silent. Shocked.

I need you to say something.

FRAN. We thought you were gay.

MARK. Right.

FRAN. Are you?

MARK. What the hell does that matter?

FRAN. I don't know.

MARK. Well, I'm not.

FRAN. Okay.

MARK. Are you relieved?

FRAN. No... no, that's not what I'm feeling right now.

MARK. What are you feeling, Mum?

FRAN. I'm... I can't... begin... Are you sure about this?

MARK. Yes.

FRAN. Then what are you feeling?

MARK. Afraid... confused... A little ashamed. No. Not ashamed. I'm finished with feeling that. But embarrassed. I guess. Telling you. And angry. Yeah. Angry. I had a whole speech prepared. I've been practising it for twenty years.

BOB. And I put my foot in it.

MARK. You did, Dad, yeah.

BOB. Are you telling us that you're one of those men who wants to be a woman?

MARK. That's the gist of it.

BOB. Is it that you like to put on women's clothing in the privacy of your own home because there was Uncle Trevor on my mother's side or are you talking about the whole shebang here?

MARK. Okay. This is something that I have known about myself for many years. It is something I have fought and hidden. It has made me very unhappy. And it has cost me a relationship with a woman I loved very much.

FRAN. Well, you can understand her point of view.

MARK. Yes, Mum. I can. Taylor's point of view is very clear.
But right now we're talking about mine… This is hard, you
know. This is so fucking hard. This was never a conversation
I wanted to have.

FRAN. It's not high on my list either.

MARK. I wanted to be normal, Mum. Whatever that is.
I wanted to grow up, get married and have my own kids.
Just like you and Dad. I wanted to love and to be loved.
That's all I ever wanted.

He looks to ROSIE *for reassurance.*

Say something, Rosie?

ROSIE. What… What should I say?

MARK. I don't know. Go read a book. Work it out for yourself.

ROSIE. Why didn't you tell me?

MARK. What?

ROSIE. I tell you everything.

MARK. I'm telling you now.

ROSIE. I thought you trusted me.

MARK. This is not about you… You understand that? Right
now, I need you to be a grown-up, Rosie.

FRAN. Stop it.

MARK. What?

FRAN. Stop thinking that we can handle this because maybe
we can't.

There is so much that needs to be said.

MARK. Okay… Yeah. Maybe I was expecting too much.
Too soon. I get that. So. I've been seeing a psychologist for a
year now. I have met people who have gone through this.
I'm ready to start hormone treatment. It's a long process but
eventually I hope to live as a woman.

FRAN. Does that involve surgery?

MARK. It might… That's a choice I'll make later.

BOB. Christ!

MARK. I'm sorry, Dad.

BOB. You could do that to your body?

MARK. This is not the right body for me.

BOB. It's the one you got. There's a reason for that.

MARK. Then whoever or whatever decides that is fucking cruel.

BOB. You can give the language a miss.

MARK. Oh, Jesus Fucking Christ!

ROSIE. Dad, it doesn't matter.

BOB. I don't know what to say to him.

MARK. You never have.

Beat – BOB *turns away.*

I've got books for you to read…

BOB. I need to think this through.

MARK. And websites for you to look up.

BOB. The wind's getting up. I should move that furniture into the shed.

BOB *retreats into the yard.*

ROSIE. Dad.

MARK. There goes my fair-weather father.

FRAN. Don't say that.

MARK. Come on, Mum. We all know that you steer this ship in a storm. He's a great dad. He coached us in the Under 15s. He was terrific at that. Anything more complex and he's a little lost.

FRAN. It might be me you see shouting the orders but it's always your father making the phone calls behind the scenes, making sure things happen. He and I are a good team. But we never saw this one coming. Don't expect us to be good at it, right away.

MARK. But eventually? Can I expect that, Mum?

She doesn't answer.

It's okay. I've got good people around me.

FRAN. What people have you got... what people have you spoken to before you would speak to your own family about this?

MARK. People like me, Mum. There's a whole world out there.

FRAN. Spare me the details, would you?

MARK. You need to get educated. If you want to have any relationship –

FRAN. What?

MARK. If you want to have a meaningful relationship –

FRAN. You're threatening me?

MARK. If you want to have a relationship with me in the future you need to know that the space in-between black and white is much wider than you have ever imagined.

FRAN. I have been a nurse for thirty years. I have seen all sorts of in-between. I have wiped the arses and tended the wounds of men who have been women and women who have been men. So I know what this looks like. But here, now I am a mother. And I'm losing something I don't want to lose. That boy. The one we raised. Your father and me. That man. What happens to him? Do we even get to say goodbye?

MARK. I'm moving to Sydney in a month.

FRAN. No.

MARK. You don't get to decide that.

FRAN. You're going to need support.

MARK. Yeah, but not from you.

They hold on each other.

I don't want to hurt you, Mum. But I can't do this here. There's no place for me here.

FRAN. We will make a place.

MARK. Yeah, I can just see it. I don't want to be the strange aunt at the end of the table at Christmas time with the stupid paper hat on her head. The woman whose hands are too large and whose voice is too deep to be right. The unhappy woman at the end of the table who everyone talks about when she goes home.

FRAN. Is that who you think we are?

MARK. Mum, I can't stay here. I've got to find my own people. I've got to make a new family.

FRAN. And what do I get? Your mother. Who pushed you out of here. My cunt. And don't flinch at the word, Mark. Not if you're going to go out and get one.

MARK. Did she just say that? Did she just do that?

FRAN. My firstborn son.

MARK. Hold on, Rosie. Because Mum is going to get mean.

FRAN. You. Yeah. You think that doesn't mean something to a mother? To me? Because I can tell you a phone call every second weekend is not going to be enough. You think you can just walk away from this? You selfish shit.

ROSIE. Mum.

FRAN. We spoilt you... You and your sister. We brought you up to think that you can have what you want, you can be what you want. No matter what the cost. Or who it hurts. People like us. Your father and me. The mugs we are. We're just the people we were told to be. And who was I told to be? A mother. Well, I wish I'd never had children.

BOB (*coming back in*). That's enough!... You need to stop before you say something you don't mean.

MARK. Too late... damage done!

BOB. Don't say that.

MARK. She's a fucking bridge burner.

BOB. Stop your swearing!… Please, I'm asking you. Both of you. To stop.

Beat.

Look, this is not easy. I don't know what to say. Maybe I never did. But this is what I know now. You're a beautiful boy. A beautiful man. You have been since you were born. You didn't get it from me. I look like I've been kicked in the face with a boot so it's your mother you've got to thank for that. Beauty and strength. You've got both. You're blessed. And now you want to mess with that. With what nature has given you. And I don't understand it… And I don't even want to. But I'm asking you not to do this.

MARK. That is too much to ask.

BOB. I'm asking, Mark. I'm asking. I've never asked for anything.

MARK. You can't ask that.

BOB. I'm asking.

MARK. Don't.

BOB. I'm begging you.

MARK. I love you, Dad. I love you both, so much. Too much. But that is too much to ask of me.

FRAN. Then go. Go on. Wear a dress if you have to. Cut your dick off if it makes you feel whole. Become the person you need to be. But not in my house. I don't want to see it. So, get out. Go. But when you come back as a woman, I will look for my son in her face and mourn his loss.

Interval.

As Winter Turns

ROSIE *is folding clothes and passing them to* MARK *as he packs a suitcase.*

MARK. It's a one-bedroom apartment… more of a bedsit really. But with rents in Sydney the way they are it's all I could afford. But at least it's on the train line and it has light. And they say that if you have light you don't need space.

ROSIE. Who says that?

MARK. People who live in bedsits, I guess.

ROSIE. I'll come up and see you.

MARK. Leave it for a while. Let me find my feet, start the treatment, you know.

ROSIE. How soon…

MARK. I have my first appointment next week.

ROSIE. And when…

MARK. I'll start to see some effects within a couple of months.

ROSIE. I'm scared that you're going to be lonely.

MARK. I'll meet people.

ROSIE. I'm worried that you're going to be unhappy.

MARK. I'm unhappy now… I have been unhappy for a long time.

ROSIE. I'm worried that people will make fun of you.

MARK. They will. Some people. Just as long as you don't.

ROSIE. I'm worried that you won't feel the same way about me.

MARK. I don't know how I'm going to feel about anything.

ROSIE. I'm worried…

MARK. Rosie… stop it.

Beat.

ROSIE. I was thinking maybe I could come up at the end of the year. That we could get a place together.

MARK. No.

ROSIE. Why not?

MARK. Because I can't be looking after you.

ROSIE. I'll look after you.

MARK. I don't want you there.

ROSIE. Why are you being so mean?

MARK. You just don't want things to change.

ROSIE. I don't know why they have to. First Pip. Now you.

MARK. You need to grow up. You need to decide who you are and get on with it. You're smart, you know. You're smarter than any of us.

ROSIE. I don't know how to do that.

MARK. You have to stop loving us so much… Mum and Dad, Pip, Ben and me. You can't love us as much as you do.

ROSIE. How do I do that?

MARK. Stop thinking that we're the best thing since sliced bread.

ROSIE. We are.

MARK. We're not. We're fucked up. Like most families.

ROSIE. I hate you.

MARK. You have to say goodbye, Rosie. You have to turn around and walk away.

ROSIE. I can't do that.

MARK. Then stay. And be the one they want.

Beat.

I don't know what I'm doing. I mean look at all this stuff. These shirts and jeans and ties and jocks. My razor and deodorant. This all belongs to somebody else now. And my watch. Rosie, Mum and Dad gave it to me for my twenty-first. It means something. I don't know what to do with all the things that mattered to me.

ROSIE. Let me wear it.

She holds out her arm. He places it on her wrist.

Hold up your arm.

MARK *holds up his arm.* ROSIE *takes off her watch, and places it around his wrist.*

What's her name?

MARK. Mia.

Transition – MARK *picks up the suitcase.*

I hear the sound of the horn and I know that it's time to go. I wish it was a taxi and that the goodbyes were over but Dad has insisted on taking me to the airport. Rosie comes too, of course. She's at the wheel. Dad is in the front passenger seat. So I sit in the back, which makes me feel like a child again, which I resent a little. Dad wants Rosie to take the coast road. She insists on taking the expressway. There is a kind of useless argument. A stand-off, that you would only tolerate with members of your own family. Rosie wins. She can be surprisingly stubborn. So we take the expressway only to discover that there are roadworks in progress so it takes longer than usual and Dad gets this 'I told you so' look on his face. And Rosie is reduced to a silent kind of rage. And I'm sitting in the back seat looking out the window thinking just how ugly the road to the airport is.

Mum is not with us. She's at work. We have hardly spoken. Our farewell was brief and hard. We both tried to outdo each other with an 'I am Still Angry With You' face. But she won. She always wins that game. But I felt the strength in her final quick embrace before she turned away and I thought it's going to be okay with her. That one day she will soften. One day she may even want to get to know… Her.

I want them to drop me at the airport and keep going. I want this goodbye to be over. I beg Rosie with my eyes. She gets it but airport farewells are still a big deal for Dad and he insists on coming inside and walking me to the gate. There is mayhem at security as he sets off the alarms. How a man can have so many pieces of metal about his person is a mystery to me but given that my time as a man is finite it's not a mystery I need to give much further thought to.

At the gate I tell Dad that I will come home soon to visit. And he tells me that he'll come to see me in Sydney as soon as I have settled in. Both of us know that neither of these things will happen but pretending they will seems to make the parting easier. I linger in his embrace knowing that it will be the last time I will be held by him, as a man, and then he does something that takes my breath away. He kisses me on the lips. And it almost does me in. It is so intimate. And I have never loved him more.

And I look back from the gate and he has broken. He is weeping. Rosie is holding him. She has him. I have to look away. I have to look ahead. I have to keep walking. My father's grief is a price I am prepared to pay.

The plane turns down the runway, increases its speed, lifts off the ground and as it makes its ascent I look down upon the city where I grew up, and steel myself against memories, against history and against the man I was. By the time I land in Sydney, Mark Price will just be someone I used to know.

Spring

Ben

The buds are bursting. There's music... there's light.

BOB *and* FRAN *are dancing. Slow, lovely, close. It's then. It's now. It's always. Their children are watching... their children are remembering... then and now.*

BEN. In the chaos of our home, in the kitchen when we were cleaning up after dinner, as arguments were being had about who did what to whom, and arrangements were being made about who had to be where when, basketball, netball, football, soccer, drama, piano, and who would take them, Mum or Dad or the bus and in the middle of the arguments about who would do what in the clean up, the washing, the drying, the putting away, and the wiping down the surfaces and who does more and who does nothing and who always goes to the toilet when the sweeping up needs to be done. (It was me.) In the midst of all this a song would come on the radio and Dad would stop and reach for her. And she would resist, she would push him off... 'I'm too busy', 'I don't have the time', 'My feet are too sore' but it was just part of their play, part of the game because she loved it when he took her, she loved it when they danced. And we, we kids, we groaned and stuck our fingers down our throats and pretended that we weren't interested, in their dancing, in their love, in the secrets that only they shared.

The children fall away, except BEN *who holds on to the memory a little longer as* BOB *and* FRAN *are left dancing. Maybe they're at the local pub or a dinner/dance at a local Surf Life Saving Club. She wears a lovely dress. Nothing too flash because she doesn't do flash and her hair is down, which it never is, and she wears her best earrings and she is beautiful. And* BOB *has his good sports jacket on and he doesn't scrub up too badly either.*

The dancing is slow, lovely, close. We think. Watching from the outside. But something else is going on. Between them. BOB *hesitates. On the inside. Asking where is she? She's not there.*

He breaks away... A moment.

FRAN. What's wrong?

BOB. I don't like the song.

FRAN. What's wrong with it?

BOB. It's too... modern.

FRAN. It's got a good beat.

BOB. Where were you?

FRAN. What?

BOB. There was a time when we danced when the only thing that was going on was you and me. Now, you're anywhere but here.

FRAN. I've got things on my mind.

BOB. What things?

FRAN. The kids.

BOB. Bugger the kids. They're not here.

FRAN. Well, that's the difference between you and me.

BOB *goes to her and kisses her on the lips.*

Have you got cancer? Is this that moment? Because I'm not ready for that.

BOB. I feel...

FRAN. Bob?

BOB. Like life has passed me by.

FRAN. You're sixty-three. There's less ahead of you than there is behind. It's terrifying. So? There's enough still to come.

BOB. For what, though?

FRAN. You and me. Whatever. All of it. Talk to me, Bob.

BOB. I'm trying.

FRAN. Try harder.

BOB. Sometimes I find myself standing in the shed wondering what to do next because everything has already been done. Everything has been watered and mulched and clipped and pruned and tied back and fertilised and all I can do is wait for the change of seasons so that I can do it all again.

FRAN. Bugger the garden.

BOB. I don't have much else.

FRAN. You stopped work too soon... I always said it.

BOB. I didn't have a choice.

FRAN. You didn't have to be among the first to take the package.

BOB. There were younger men. And women. Much younger. With small children. They needed the work more than I did.

FRAN. You should have found something else.

BOB. I was fifty-six... No one wanted me.

FRAN. Other men weren't so quick to throw in the towel.

BOB. Is that what you think I did?

FRAN. Didn't you?

BOB. I thought...

FRAN. What?

BOB. I don't know... I thought I had earned it. The rest. The leisure. Now, there's a word for a man who's worked since he was sixteen. Leisure. Christ, when I worked all I could dream of was a few extra hours in the day to spend in the garden but who would have thought that the days would turn out to be so long.

FRAN. Stop it!

BOB. What?

FRAN. I don't want you to be old, Bob. (*Pointing to her head.*) In here. There's plenty of time for that. Later. Wait for me. We'll do it together but not yet.

BOB. Well, how do you fend it off... Tell me? I feel a weight on me, Fran. Sixty-three years is bloody heavy.

FRAN. We'll go away.

BOB. Away?

FRAN. A change. Something different. We'll go to Europe. Or the Caribbean.

BOB. Overseas?

FRAN. Why not?

BOB. With what?

FRAN. We'll find it. When we need it. We always have.

BOB. Away, you reckon?

FRAN. Other people do it. Why not us?

BOB. Well... I've always wanted to go the Kruger National Park. In South Africa.

FRAN. Then we'll go.

BOB. It's probably too expensive.

FRAN. Bob... We'll find it. We will. But right now this is what's going to happen. You and me are going home and we're going to get beneath the sheets and have a good go at it.

BOB. Well, that could put a spring back in my step, I suppose.

FRAN. I want to be bounced around a bit, Bob. Flipped over and turned upside down, like the old days.

BOB. I can't promise that. It's the knees, love.

FRAN. Then we'll do it face to face. Eye to eye. Whatever works. But we're going to have sex and we're going to remember who we are, Bob Price.

Home

That Night

BEN. Where's Mum and Dad?

ROSIE. Out.

BEN. Where?

ROSIE. It's their anniversary.

BEN. I need to see them.

ROSIE. Ben, what's wrong?

BEN. Did you hear a car?

ROSIE. I don't think so.

BEN. Maybe it's them.

ROSIE. I didn't hear anything.

BEN. I want Mum.

ROSIE. Are you on something?

BEN. No.

ROSIE. Are you?

BEN. No.

ROSIE. Don't come here if you're on something. It's their anniversary. It's not fair.

BEN. I'm not on anything.

ROSIE. You're sweating, Ben.

BEN. I've been running.

ROSIE. Running? Where?

BEN. Running and running.

ROSIE. Where?

BEN. I'm so tired, Rosie.

ROSIE. Okay.

BEN. I've been running.

ROSIE. I know.

BEN. Was that a car?

ROSIE. No.

BEN. I need Mum.

ROSIE. They're out.

BEN. Can you phone them?

ROSIE. You want a cup of tea?

BEN. I've been running, Rosie.

ROSIE. Something to eat?

BEN. I've been running.

ROSIE. You're home. You're here. You don't have to run any more.

BEN. You don't understand. This is what I've been running from. I've been running. And running. And look where I end up. I'm so angry.

ROSIE. Don't be.

BEN. I could fuckin' –

ROSIE. Don't.

BEN. I could fuckin' hit something.

ROSIE. Don't.

BEN. I'm frightened, Rosie.

ROSIE. So am I.

FRAN *enters*.

FRAN. What's going on?

ROSIE *says it all with her eyes*.

Ben? Look at me?

BOB *enters*.

Look at me?

BOB. What's going on?

FRAN. Have you taken something?

BEN. No.

FRAN. Your eyes.

BEN. I'm tired.

FRAN. Your pupils are enlarged.

BEN. I've been running.

FRAN. Okay. It's all right. You're going to be all right. But I need to know what you're on.

BOB. Is he on drugs?

She feels his temperature.

FRAN. You're burning.

BOB. Have you come into this house on drugs?

FRAN. Leave it, Bob.

BOB. I want an answer.

BEN. What do you want to know, Mr Nap-a-Lot?

BOB. What drugs have you taken?

FRAN. Maybe leave it, Bob. Until he's calm.

BOB. I bloody well won't leave it. You're in my house, boy.

BEN. Mum?

FRAN. Don't provoke him, Bob.

BOB. Rosie, what's he taken?

ROSIE. I don't know.

BOB. You've frightened your sister... And your mother. What have you got to say for yourself?

BEN. What do you want to know?

BOB. I want to know what drugs you've taken.

BEN. It's easier to ask me what drugs I haven't taken.

That's a red rag to a bull... BOB *is taking his jacket off and squaring off in a flash.*

BOB. That's it. I should have taken you in hand years ago.

FRAN (*simultaneous*). No, Bob!

ROSIE (*simultaneous*). Dad!

BOB. Come on... Come on... I'll take you on.

BEN. You're going to hit me?

FRAN. Ben, don't you dare touch him.

BEN. I'm not. He's trying to hit me.

FRAN. No one's hitting anyone.

BOB. Get out of the way, woman.

ROSIE. Dad, you can't fight him.

BEN. This is not about drugs. Dad! Please! I need you. I've done something really bad.

Everybody stops.

I've stolen some money.

FRAN *goes to say something but* BOB *holds up his hand to silence her.*

BOB. Go on.

BEN. I've been skimming.

BOB. Which is?

BEN. I move money. Lots of it. Every day. It's possible to skim a little off the top and to direct it to a bogus account. If you're the one who inputs the data. If it's done in small amounts and at irregular intervals it's difficult to trace.

BOB. How long has it been going on?

BEN. About eighteen months. I got greedy. I got lazy. I kept taking. There's an internal investigation. It's going to come my way very soon.

BOB. Are we talking about a lot of money?

BEN. That depends on what kind of world you live in.

BOB. How much?

BEN. Around two hundred and fifty.

BOB. Thousand, right? Two hundred and fifty thousand.

BEN *nods.*

In what world is that not a lot of money? It's not a world that we live in. When did you go there? To that world?

BEN. I don't know. Mum?

BOB. She can't help you. She can't solve this one.

BEN. Mum?

BOB. What part of you doesn't understand that stealing is wrong?

BEN. Yeah, all right.

BOB. It's black and white, isn't it?

BEN. Dad, I can't cop a lecture now, right?

BOB. A lecture from me is the least of what's coming your way. So answer me. It's black and white, right?

FRAN. Bob.

BOB. Shut up, Fran. For once. Shut up! Is it black and white, Ben?

BEN. Yes.

BOB. You know the difference between right and wrong. You couldn't have grown up in this house without knowing that.

BEN. Yes.

BOB. So you knew you were doing the wrong thing.

BEN. Yes.

BOB. And you did it anyway?

BEN. Yes... yes!

BOB. Then why?

BEN. Because I could.

BOB. Do you hear that, Fran? Our son stole money because
he could.

BEN. Listen.

BOB. It better be good.

BEN. I started hanging out with a different kind of people.
People who earned more. Had more. The private-school boys.
Rich. Safe. And paid for. You've got no idea what these people
have. I wanted to be one of them. You know, they just assume
that you've got what they've got. And if they find out you
haven't they don't want to know you. You're out. You're
looking at their backs before you even know it.

BOB. Am I meant to be moved by that?

BEN. Mum?

BOB. Am I meant to feel sorry for you?

FRAN. Okay, Bob.

BOB. Poor little boy with the working-class parents found
himself on the other side of town. What did you tell them
when they asked you what school you went to, Ben? What
did you tell them when they asked what your parents did for
a living? My old man works on a car assembly plant? How
dare you think that this is not good enough? Who the hell are
you? Who even let you into this house?

He goes for him. FRAN *and* ROSIE *intervene.*

FRAN (*simultaneous*). No, Bob.

ROSIE (*simultaneous*). Stop it, Dad.

BEN. Hit me, old man... come on, hit me.

BEN *starts hitting himself in the face.* FRAN *and* ROSIE
leave BOB *to hold* BEN *and stop him from hurting himself.*

FRAN (*simultaneous*). Stop it. Don't.

ROSIE (*simultaneous*). Ben.

In the fracas, BEN *raises a fist to strike his mother. It shocks them all to stillness and silence.*

A moment.

FRAN. Right. The first thing that is going to happen is that you're going to pay back the money.

BEN. I don't have it.

BOB. No. Of course you don't. Some of it is sitting in the driveway. We'll sell that. That's a start. And a fair whack of it probably went up your nose. Can't get that back.

FRAN. We'll take out a mortgage on the house.

BOB. We bloody well will not.

FRAN. Bob… please.

BOB. Have you forgotten? A thirty-year mortgage paid back in sixteen?

FRAN. How could I?

BOB. What that cost us?

FRAN. I know.

BOB. The double shifts? The overtime? The holidays not taken? Years of doing without. Why? Because we thought being debt free meant something. We thought it meant we were good people.

FRAN. He's stolen from people… He could go to jail.

BOB. That's right.

BEN. Dad, I'll pay you back.

BOB. With what wage? You're not going to have a job by the morning and nobody employs a thief. No. You'll need two signatures on the paperwork, Fran, and you're not getting mine.

FRAN. All right then… I've got the money.

BOB. What money?

FRAN. I've got some put aside.

ROSIE. No, Mum.

BOB. What money?

FRAN. I've put some aside. Over the years. It's not quite what he owes but it's close to it.

BOB. That much?

She nods.

You've kept that much aside?

FRAN. Yes.

BOB. From me?

FRAN. Yes.

ROSIE. It was a surprise, Dad.

BOB. Well, it's certainly that, love. It's a big surprise.

BEN. There's a chance that if I can put it right with them they won't go to the police.

BOB. Why's that?

BEN. Look, they work on the margins as it is. You know what I'm saying? They won't want the cops all over their books. If I can put this right…

BOB. It's not going to happen that way, Ben. First thing in the morning we're going to your boss and you're going to tell him what you've done.

BEN. I'm not the only one at it.

BOB. You might want to mention that as well.

BEN. It's not that easy.

BOB. Yes it is. You just stick a whistle in your mouth and blow. After that we're going to the police station.

FRAN. But if we can put this right.

BOB. There's only one way to do that and that's to let the boy
face the consequences of what he's done.

FRAN. You're going to ruin his life.

BOB. He did that with the first dollar he took that wasn't his.
You let something ugly in, son. Envy. No. You're going to
take responsibility for what you've done even if it means jail.

BEN. Fuck that!

BOB. No fuck you! Fuck you! Fuck you! For bringing this
into our home. The opportunities you've been given.
To finish school. To go to university. What I could have
done with an opportunity like that. But you! You get a
degree in accountancy so that you can steal from people.
So no! Fuck you!

FRAN goes into the garden.

BEN. Dad, I'm scared.

BOB. You should be. Now give me your keys… Do I have to
take them off you?

BEN hands BOB his keys.

Right… you'll sleep here tonight.

BOB heads outside.

BEN. Dad?

BOB (*looking back*). I've got nothing for you, Ben. No words
to reassure you. No hug to make you feel better. What I had,
I've already given. And you never wanted it anyway.

He moves outside to join FRAN. A moment.

So, he's not the only one who's been doing some skimming,
then.

FRAN. It was mine. My wage. I earned it.

BOB. Right. It's just that every pay packet I ever earned went
straight into a bank account with both our names on it. There
was never a mine. Just ours.

FRAN. It was my 'Get Out' money, Bob. I saw it happen to my
    mother. Stuck in a miserable marriage with a man she didn't
    love because she couldn't afford to leave. It wasn't going to
    happen to me. So, I put a little away. Every pay. Until I had
    enough to buy some shares.

BOB. Shares!

FRAN. Mining. Iron ore. The price goes through the roof and
    suddenly I'm a wealthy woman. I start to get nervous. I read
    the papers. I can see what's coming so I sell. And then the
    price goes down. I played it well.

BOB. Right.

FRAN. I'm not justifying it... I don't have to.

BOB. No. But a man wouldn't mind an explanation why he
    wasn't let in on it.

FRAN. I told you... I had to know I could go if I ever needed to.

BOB. Did you... Ever need to?

    Her silence is the answer.

    What stopped you?

FRAN. The children. I stayed because of the kids.

BOB. And me? Where was I in this picture?

FRAN. You can't love someone for thirty years straight. You
    fall out of love. Or there's no time for love. Or love is not the
    point. Getting by is the point. Raising children is the point.
    I'll stop if you don't want to hear this.

BOB. No... I want to know.

FRAN. You fall out of love. You just do. And you think about,
    maybe, something else. Another life. But it passes. If you
    wait long enough, one day you realise that the man you did
    love is still there, still sitting across the table from you, still
    sleeping on the other side of the bed. And you settle for that.

BOB. You settled for me.

FRAN. I'm being honest, Bob.

BOB. Was there ever someone else?

FRAN. Don't ask me that.

BOB. Was there?

FRAN. I don't want to hurt you.

BOB. Was there?

FRAN. There was someone who wanted me.

BOB. And?

FRAN. I said no.

BOB. Did you love him?

FRAN. For a moment.

BOB. Who was he?

FRAN. Does that matter?

BOB. I'm not sure.

FRAN. He was a patient. Long term. I cared for him. We had
   some time, you know, to get to know one another... He liked
   Leonard Cohen.

   A moment.

   I chose you. You and the kids. And what we had.

BOB. And regretted it ever since.

FRAN. No.

BOB. Yeah. You punished me, Fran. You punished us. Pip
   especially. With your fury. With your screaming out at the
   unfairness of it all. Married... With four kids. One you
   weren't expecting. An accident. You thought you were done.
   You had other plans. That was about the time wasn't it?
   When some other bloke wanted you? Funny what a husband
   will do to make sure his wife stays.

FRAN. You knew?

BOB. A man's not blind to his wife's unhappiness.

FRAN. So you thought a kid would fix it?

BOB. The kid happened... and I'm glad of it. Unless...

FRAN. Don't.

BOB. You're going to break my heart if you tell me that girl is not mine.

FRAN. You're Rosie's father.

BOB. I'm the man who brought her up, I know that much.

*She could hurt him with a lie or save him with the truth.
Or is it the other way around?*

FRAN. I never slept with him. I could have. He wanted me. I lay with him a few times. Late at night. Held him. Let him hold me. That was enough. And more than I was getting from you at the time. He asked me to go away with him. Me? Never had a man ask me such a thing. I thought about it. For a moment. A day. A week. And then I said no.

BOB. And settled for me.

FRAN. That's about it, yeah.

BOB. You're too hard, Fran... You want to learn how to give a man a way back.

Beat.

FRAN. I won't stand by and watch Ben go to jail. Not if I can help it. You need to know that.

BOB. It's your money, so do what you want with it. But what you give to Ben you have to give to the other three. I won't have one child favoured financially.

FRAN. It won't leave much over for you and me.

BOB. You and me?

Summer

Rosie

The roses are back in bloom. A year has passed since ROSIE *returned from Europe. Everything is the same and yet so much has changed.*

ROSIE *snaps a rose from its stem. She plucks a few petals and lets them fall.* FRAN *is watching her.*

FRAN. You'll break your father's heart.

ROSIE. Don't say that.

FRAN. Well?

ROSIE. What about yours? Will I break yours?

FRAN. No. I'm ready for you to go. I'm over being a mother.

ROSIE. I don't want you to be over me.

FRAN. Out of sight. Out of mind.

ROSIE. You don't mean that.

BOB *enters.*

BOB. Rosie, you've parked too close to the wall. I can't get my wheelbarrow through. I've told you a hundred times.

ROSIE. I'll shift it.

FRAN. Rosie's got something to tell you.

ROSIE. It can wait until later.

FRAN. No, it can't.

BOB. What is it?

FRAN. She's leaving.

ROSIE. Mum!

FRAN. She's enrolled in a course.

BOB. A course! Well, that's good. Isn't it? In what?

FRAN. Go on.

ROSIE. It's a creative writing course.

BOB *looks to* FRAN.

FRAN. I know, I told her.

BOB. Well, how are you going to earn a living from that?

FRAN. That's what I said.

BOB. Maybe you should think about getting a qualification first.

FRAN. Like nursing.

BOB. Or teaching.

FRAN. Or journalism.

BOB. Now, that sounds like something worth looking at.

ROSIE. No.

BOB. Just something you can

FRAN. Fall back on. That's what I said.

BOB. In case the creative writing doesn't

FRAN. Work out which it probably won't.

ROSIE. Mum!

FRAN. Well, you might not be any good at it.

ROSIE. Yeah but let me find that out… This is not something I've just made up because I don't know what else to do. I have to try this. I think if I don't I will regret it.

BOB. Well, where is this course?

ROSIE. At Griffith University.

BOB. Griffith? Griffith? Where's that? Do I know that one?

FRAN. It's in Brisbane.

BOB. Brisbane! Could you have chosen any place further away?

ROSIE. It's got a good reputation.

BOB. But you don't know anyone in Brisbane.

ROSIE. I know. Isn't it great?

BOB. Well, who do we know in Brisbane, Fran?

FRAN. No one.

BOB. What about…

FRAN. No.

BOB. The couple that used to live two doors down. Didn't they move to Brisbane?

FRAN. The Turners. We don't know them.

BOB. But we did. We used to have them over. And go to theirs.

FRAN. Twenty years ago, Bob.

BOB. But we could give them a call. At least it's someone. You can't just go somewhere where you don't know anyone. You need somewhere to stay until you find your feet.

ROSIE. I've arranged to stay on someone's couch until I find somewhere.

BOB. Fran?

FRAN. It's what they do, Bob.

BOB. Well, when is all this happening?

ROSIE. I'll drive up in about three weeks.

BOB. Drive!

ROSIE. I'll need a car up there.

BOB. You're throwing a lot of balls at me at once here, Rosie. I don't think you've thought this through. We could put it on a truck. Have it sent up.

ROSIE. I want to do the drive. I'm going to stop in Sydney and see Mia.

BOB. Well, here's an idea. How about I drive up with you. Then fly back. We'll make a trip out of it. A father and daughter thing. I won't talk too much if that's what you're worried about. And you can listen to your music... When the news isn't on. Fran, what do you think about that idea?

ROSIE *pleads for help with a look to her mum.*

FRAN. Not this time, Bob.

BOB. But it's such a long way. And you're not used to driving long distances.

FRAN. Bob.

BOB. There're trucks on the highway. Have you seen how fast they go? And they take up the whole road, Rosie. You've got no idea. They won't even see you in that bug of a car you drive.

ROSIE. I'll toot.

BOB. You don't even know what road to take to get out of Adelaide. So how the hell will you get to Brisbane?

ROSIE. Don't cry, Dad.

BOB. I'm not.

ROSIE. You're going to make me cry.

BOB. I'm not crying.

They both are.

ROSIE. I had to go sooner or later.

BOB. Yeah, but so far... did you have to go so far?

ROSIE. You can't make this so hard for me. You have to help me do this, Dad. This is normal. This is what's meant to happen.

ROSIE *flees before she breaks and backs down.*

(*As she exits.*) I'll shift my car.

BOB. Not her, Fran.

FRAN. I know.

BOB. Not her.

FRAN. What are you talking about? Were you going to hang on to her for the rest of her life?

BOB. It wasn't meant to be like this… I thought they'd be like us. But better than us. Better versions of us. Better educated. With better jobs. And better prospects. That's what we worked so hard for. Wasn't it? But I thought they'd all live close by. In the same city, at least. In a house they built. Just like us. And that they'd get married to good people. And have kids. Like us. And that we'd put on a barbecue here most Sundays. And there would be all the kids. All the cousins. And that there'd be cricket. And totem tennis. And sleepovers at Nan and Pop's. You know. And engagements. And weddings. Here in this garden. I thought that's what life would be. That's all I ever wanted it to be, Fran.

Life Goes On

BOB *is pushing a load of dirt across the backyard. He stops…*
lost for a moment. FRAN *is on her way to work.*

FRAN. Bob… Bob… BOB!

BOB. What?

FRAN. I was talking to you.

BOB. I know.

FRAN. Where are you?

BOB. I'm here, Fran. I've always been here.

FRAN. I've done a pasta bake for Steve and the kids. He's
    picking it up on his way home from work. And there're some
    chops in the fridge for you. I'm going.

BOB. Good.

FRAN. I'm working late.

BOB. Don't wake me.

FRAN. Text me if you hear from Rosie.

BOB. I will.

FRAN. You told her to stop off, didn't you?

BOB. In Narrandera, if she got that far.

FRAN. So text me when you hear from her.

BOB. I said I would.

FRAN. Straight away. Because I'll be waiting.

BOB. What's wrong with you?

FRAN. What?

BOB. Why are you always so angry?

FRAN. I'm not.

BOB. You are… you always have been.

FRAN. I'm not angry… I'm tired. There's always so much to do and I'm always running late and I'm worried about Rosie being on the road alone and… I'm just tired, Bob.

BOB. Then stop. There's nothing more to do. They've all gone.

They hold on one another… the space between them that their children once filled is enormous.

FRAN. Did I do this? Did I drive them away?

He could hurt her with the truth or save her with a lie. Or is it the other way around?

BOB. They've made their own choices, Fran.

She nods, grateful for his kindness.

FRAN. I thought we could make a few changes out here.

BOB. Hey?

FRAN. We could make a little more room. Pull up some of the lawn and maybe get rid of some roses.

BOB. The roses!

FRAN. We could plant some other things. Like natives.

BOB. Natives!

FRAN. I want to plant some vines and creepers, and herbs. Things that grow every which way and all over the place and on top of each other. I want a garden full of chaos and mess and places where you can hide and get away when you need to.

BOB. Well, I suppose we could do something with that patch behind the shed.

FRAN. No, Bob. I'm talking about tearing up the whole lot of it and starting again… Text me when you hear from her.

She leaves… BOB *is alone in the garden. He looks up at the eucalypt and listens to the rustle of the leaves in the wind.*

And It Ends Like This

A telephone is ringing.

BOB *enters in his pyjamas and bare feet. He stares at the phone. His children are watching… then, now, always.*

The phone rings once… twice… three times… four times. BOB *answers.*

BOB. Hello.

PIP. You didn't see it coming.

BEN. It hits you like a blow to the back of the head.

MIA. Like a punch in the stomach.

BEN. Like a kick to the back of the knees.

PIP. You almost don't recognise the name.

MIA. It's like they're talking about someone else.

BEN. Someone you don't know.

MIA. Because you never thought it was possible.

BEN. Never even imagined it.

PIP. A world

MIA. A life

BEN. Without her.

    A moment.

ROSIE. Her shift finished at 3 a.m. She was in the car and on the road by 3:05. She was tired. It had been a difficult shift, the usual shortage of beds and juggling of patients but they had also lost someone that night. A woman she had let herself get close to. She had allowed herself a moment's reflection on the passing of time before she steeled herself against it and got on with the night.

She was travelling down the expressway. She was tired. She was thinking about her kids. She was worried about me, being on the road alone, wondering if I'd get there alive, forcing herself not to think the worst but thinking it anyway. She was worried about Pip. She felt guilty that she had still not answered her letter. But she wasn't much of a writer and wasn't sure that she could say what Pip needed to hear, anyway. She was worried about Mia. She regretted the things that were said between them and the coldness of their parting. She felt her bottom lip quiver when she thought of her alone in Sydney. She'll call her in the morning, just to hear her voice. She was still cross with Ben. And found a way to let him know it on most days of the week. She wondered if she had been too soft with him and let him get away with things that she wouldn't have stood for from the others.

She thought about love and how sometimes you could give too much and sometimes you couldn't give enough and that knowing the right place in-between wasn't easy. And she thought about Bob. He'll still be asleep. She looked forward to crawling into bed beside him. She loved the warmth of him in the morning.

She was thinking of all this when her eyes closed, just for a moment. She veered off the inside lane and hit the concrete divider before flipping the car. She was crushed on impact. She was dead on arrival at the hospital where she worked.

PIP. I'll catch the

MIA. I'm on my

BEN. I'll be there

ALL. Dad?

> BOB *puts the phone down. He moves out to the garden. He looks up to the sky. And then he breaks with rage and tears the rose bushes from the ground until his hands are shredded and covered in blood and the roses lie strewn across the lawn.*

PIP. I hang up. I pull back the curtains. It's snowing. Everything is white. And suddenly I feel so cold and so far away. Please, God. Not her. I think about phoning him and asking him to come, instead I reach for my laptop and start searching for a flight. And I know that this, whatever this is, is over and that I have to go home.

MIA. I hang up. I open the window. The heat and noise hit me in the face. I can hear a train passing nearby and a couple having sex in the flat below. I want to scream. I want to cry. Please, God. Not her. This can't be happening. There is so much that still needs to be said.

BEN. I hang up. I walk. I stumble. I fall. Not her. Please, God. Not her. I cry. I weep. I bash my head on the floor. Not her. Please, God. Not her.

During the next, PIP, MIA *and* BEN (*who are already dressed for their mother's funeral*) *approach* BOB *and wash the mud and blood from his hands and face. They take off his pyjamas and dress him in a suit and shirt and tie and shoes and socks. They brush his hair. They are so tender with him.*

ROSIE. I hang up. I get out of the car. I can hardly breathe. I'm standing on the side of the highway. I don't know whether to turn back or to keep going. I'm somewhere between who I was and who I'm going to be. I want my dad. I want my sisters and brother. I want my mum. I want my mum. But I can't think of her, of them, not now, because if I do my chest will explode. I feel like I'm literally going to fall to pieces. That my arms are going to drop off and then my legs and my head. And so to stop myself coming apart I make a list of all the things I know to be true.

I know that having your heart broken by a boy from Spain won't be the worst thing that happens to you. I know that things can't remain the same no matter how much you want them to. I know that people aren't perfect. Even the people you love. Especially the people you love. And I know that love is not enough to save them.

I know what grief tastes like. It's bitter. I know what it sounds like. It's loud. And I know that on the day my mother died my childhood finally ended.

I know that summer turns to autumn and that autumn becomes winter and that winter turns to spring and spring back to summer. And it goes on.

Life.

It goes on.

She joins BOB *and the other children. There's a moment between the five of them. There are no words to be said. Just touch. Just silence. A moment. Together. Until something practical can be found to grasp on to.*

BEN. The car's here.

BOB. Are we ready?

PIP. I think so.

BOB. Right then... Let's go.

They hold hands as they leave... whatever seems right between them.

BOB *hesitates as the children go on. He looks back to the garden.*

But she's not there.

The End.

Other Titles in this Series

Mike Bartlett
ALBION
BULL
GAME
AN INTERVENTION
KING CHARLES III
WILD

Stephen Beresford
THE LAST OF THE HAUSSMANS

Andrew Bovell
SPEAKING IN TONGUES
WHEN THE RAIN STOPS FALLING

Jake Brunger
FOUR PLAY

Melissa Bubnic
BEACHED
BOYS WILL BE BOYS

Jez Butterworth
THE FERRYMAN
JERUSALEM
JEZ BUTTERWORTH PLAYS: ONE
MOJO
THE NIGHT HERON
PARLOUR SONG
THE RIVER
THE WINTERLING

Alexi Kaye Campbell
ALEXI KAYE CAMPBELL PLAYS: ONE
APOLOGIA
BRACKEN MOOR
THE FAITH MACHINE
THE PRIDE
SUNSET AT THE VILLA THALIA

Caryl Churchill
BLUE HEART
CHURCHILL PLAYS: THREE
CHURCHILL PLAYS: FOUR
CHURCHILL: SHORTS
CLOUD NINE
DING DONG THE WICKED
A DREAM PLAY *after* Strindberg
DRUNK ENOUGH TO SAY
    I LOVE YOU?
ESCAPED ALONE
FAR AWAY
HERE WE GO
HOTEL
ICECREAM
LIGHT SHINING IN
    BUCKINGHAMSHIRE
LOVE AND INFORMATION
MAD FOREST
A NUMBER
PIGS AND DOGS
SEVEN JEWISH CHILDREN
THE SKRIKER
THIS IS A CHAIR
THYESTES *after* Seneca
TRAPS

Declan Greene
MOTH

Vicky Jones
THE ONE
TOUCHED

Lucy Kirkwood
BEAUTY AND THE BEAST
    with Katie Mitchell
BLOODY WIMMIN
THE CHILDREN
CHIMERICA
HEDDA *after* Ibsen
IT FELT EMPTY WHEN THE
    HEART WENT AT FIRST BUT
    IT IS ALRIGHT NOW
LUCY KIRKWOOD PLAYS: ONE
MOSQUITOES
NSFW
TINDERBOX

Tommy Murphy
HOLDING THE MAN
STRANGERS IN BETWEEN

Joanne Murray-Smith
BOMBSHELLS
THE FEMALE OF THE SPECIES
HONOUR

Luke Norris
GOODBYE TO ALL THAT
GROWTH
SO HERE WE ARE

Evan Placey
CONSENSUAL
GIRLS LIKE THAT
GIRLS LIKE THAT & OTHER PLAYS
    FOR TEENAGERS
PRONOUN

Stef Smith
GIRL IN THE MACHINE
HUMAN ANIMALS
REMOTE
SWALLOW

Jack Thorne
2ND MAY 1997
BUNNY
BURYING YOUR BROTHER IN
    THE PAVEMENT
HOPE
JACK THORNE PLAYS: ONE
JUNKYARD
LET THE RIGHT ONE IN
    after John Ajvide Lindqvist
MYDIDAE
THE SOLID LIFE OF SUGAR WATER
STACY & FANNY AND FAGGOT
WHEN YOU CURE ME
WOYZECK *after* Büchner

Phoebe Waller-Bridge
FLEABAG

'A great published script makes you understand what the play is, at its heart' *Slate Magazine*

Enjoyed this book? Choose from hundreds more classic and contemporary plays from Nick Hern Books, the UK's leading independent theatre publisher.

Our full range is available to browse online now, including:

Award-winning plays from leading contemporary dramatists, including *King Charles III* by Mike Bartlett, *Anne Boleyn* by Howard Brenton, *Jerusalem* by Jez Butterworth, *A Breakfast of Eels* by Robert Holman, *Chimerica* by Lucy Kirkwood, *The Night Alive* by Conor McPherson, *The James Plays* by Rona Munro, *Nell Gwynn* by Jessica Swale, and many more…

Ground-breaking drama from the most exciting up-and-coming playwrights, including Vivienne Franzmann, James Fritz, Ella Hickson, Anna Jordan, Jack Thorne, Phoebe Waller-Bridge, Tom Wells, and many more…

Twentieth-century classics, including *Cloud Nine* by Caryl Churchill, *Death and the Maiden* by Ariel Dorfman, *Pentecost* by David Edgar, *Angels in America* by Tony Kushner, *Long Day's Journey into Night* by Eugene O'Neill, *The Deep Blue Sea* by Terence Rattigan, *Machinal* by Sophie Treadwell, and many more…

Timeless masterpieces from playwrights throughout the ages, including Anton Chekhov, Euripides, Henrik Ibsen, Federico García Lorca, Christopher Marlowe, Molière, William Shakespeare, Richard Brinsley Sheridan, Oscar Wilde, and many more…

Every playscript is a world waiting to be explored. Find yours at **www.nickhernbooks.co.uk** – you'll receive a 20% discount, plus free UK postage & packaging for orders over £30.

'Publishing plays gives permanent form to an evanescent art, and allows many more people to have some kind of experience of a play than could ever see it in the theatre' *Nick Hern, publisher*

www.nickhernbooks.co.uk

A Nick Hern Book

Things I Know To Be True first published in Great Britain as a paperback original in 2016 by Nick Hern Books Limited, The Glasshouse, 49a Goldhawk Road, London W12 8QP, in association with Frantic Assembly and State Theatre Company of South Australia

Reprinted in this revised edition 2017

Things I Know To Be True copyright © 2016, 2017 Andrew Bovell

Andrew Bovell has asserted his right to be identified as the author of this work

'Famous Blue Raincoat' words and music by Leonard Cohen. © Copyright Chrysalis Songs Ltd. Permission granted via Hal Leonard Australia Pty Ltd, ABN 13 085 333 713, www.halleonard.com.au. Used By Permission. All Rights Reserved. Unauthorised Reproduction is Illegal.

Cover image by Feast Creative

Designed and typeset by Nick Hern Books, London
Printed and bound in Great Britain by CPI Group (UK) Ltd

A CIP catalogue record for this book is available from the British Library

ISBN   978 1 84842 576 7

MIX
Paper from
responsible sources
FSC® C020471

www.nickhernbooks.co.uk

facebook.com/nickhernbooks

twitter.com/nickhernbooks